HIGH ENDEAVOUR

HIGH ENDEAVOUR

The Life of Air Chief Marshal
Sir Ronald Ivelaw-Chapman,
GCB, KBE, DFC, AFC

by
John Ivelaw-Chapman

LEO COOPER
LONDON

First published in Great Britain in 1993 by
LEO COOPER.
an imprint of
Pen & Sword Books Ltd,
47 Church Street, Barnsley, South Yorkshire S70 2AS

A CIP catalogue record for this book is available from the British Library

ISBN 0 85052 316 8

Typeset by Yorkshire Web, Barnsley, South Yorkshire
in Plantin 10 point

Printed by
Redwood Books,
Trowbridge, Wiltshire

CONTENTS

DEDICATION

To my Mother,
Lady Ivelaw-Chapman

ACKNOWLEDGEMENT

I am much indebted to Anne Baker for kindly allowing me to quote extracts from *Wings Over Kabul* (William Kimber, 1975), which she wrote in conjuction with my father.

INTRODUCTION

Air Chief Marshal Sir Ronald Ivelaw-Chapman, GCB, KBE, DFC, AFC, died of abdominal cancer in May 1978. For three years he knew of his approaching death as a strong possibility. It was an inescapable certainty for the last three months. During his final years he seems to have been overtaken by a compulsion to share with other people the history of his remarkable life. He was not a boastful man, nor conceited, just somehow grateful, yet he could never overcome his innate serviceman's reticence. He was scornful of his military contemporaries for whom the 'Bubble Reputation' became an obsession in retirement, and for as long as I remember, even after the most convivial dinner, he never recounted anything that might have been described as an exploit or needlessly 'dropped' a famous name.

My father was a compulsive archivist. In the mahogany wardrobe in his dressing room there were leather collar boxes and starched mess kit shirts, suits with waistcoats, braces, sock suspenders and a lifetime's collection of ties that meant something. At the bottom of the wardrobe, partially hidden by highly polished shoes and boots, could be found the archives; a wondrous collection of papers and photographs, ephemera and souvenirs, all bound, bundled and annotated like the contents of a deed box. As a boy, when exploring unsupervised this treasure trove, I remember uncovering a Luftwaffe officer's sword, and for a while among the papers there was an unlicensed service revolver with ten rounds of ammunition carefully wrapped in oiled silk. He found a new hiding place for this once he realized, in disapproving silence, that the security of the wardrobe had been breached.

To complement the five volumes of annotated scrapbooks and the numerous photo albums there were two slim, black looseleaf volumes, amateurishly typed, with their titles carefully sellotaped to the outer covers: *Memories and Musings* by R. Ivelaw-Chapman, Part 1 and Part 2. These amounted almost to a confessional — the private thoughts of a retired Air Chief Marshal who was unusually introspective and self-critical. The *Memories* pages were filled with wonderful anecdotes and recollections, but the *Musings* set out a sadly well-worn philosophy, and when I read the uninspiring but meticulous prose I was at first slightly embarrassed by the very ordinariness of the conclusions that were so carefully argued. He set down his views on Social Security, Matrimony, Capital Punishment, the

Malaise of Britain and many such well-chewed bones of contention, but his opinions were hackneyed; very little was original or far-sighted.

Why, I wondered, was it important for him to set down all these rather conventional musings when the number of words that he still had time to write was so sadly limited? "Tell us," I wish I could have urged him, "what it was like over the First World War battlefields in a string-bag biplane. Did your guts turn to water when you knew that your Lancaster was burning from end to end and there was fifteen thousand feet of nothing between you and the dark and hostile French countryside below? Did Nehru try to outstare you when you told him that you would resign as Commander-in-Chief before allowing the Indian Air Force to launch a pre-emptive strike against Pakistan?" That, surely, is the stuff of biographies. But there was little of this and what there was lay between the precisely ruled and regimentally paragraphed lines.

The introduction to *Memories and Musings*, which I will refer to as 'The Biographical Notes', reads as follows:

I have often admired and envied the skill of the autobiographer who has knit together a narrative of his life with thoughts and ideas that have most influenced him during his lifetime. I have neither the skill nor the power of expression to make an account of my life interesting to my friends, much less the general public.

Yet in a way I have had quite an eventful innings. Moreover my ideas on what really matters in life have changed so fundamentally from age 17 to 75 that it has struck me as being a good piece of mental discipline to force myself, despite my inept pen, to commit to paper some of the thoughts and ideas that have coloured my life these past 6 or 7 decades. I could not hope to weave these Memories and Musings *into a chronological story, so, instead, I have set them down in separate and unconnected chapters. I have also interjected a collection of anecdotes which may help to fill in some of the gaps in the sketchy narrative of my life in the Royal Air Force and after I retired from it. Disjointed though the result may be, I hope that some day it will bring a smile or two to the lips of my immediate progeny and of my grandchildren.*

> R. Ivelaw-Chapman
> Knockwood,
> Nether Wallop,
> Hampshire.
> 1975.

It is a discipline within the armed forces that everything that is written down, be it an operation order, a service paper or even a letter should conform to a standard layout and should have an introduction, a body and a conclusion; and somewhere between the introduction and the body should be stated the Aim.

The Aim is much exalted in the Services. "The Aim should state as clearly and concisely as possible the object of an undertaking. It is always written down as much to clarify the writer's thought process as to instruct the reader." Aims are permitted to be modified in Time and Space only and should always start with an infinitive: ie. "To eliminate enemy forces ON the airfield at Dar es Salaam BEFORE first light ON the 2nd February comma 1961." It was a mortal sin to omit the comma.

So, Sir R. Ivelaw-Chapman, retired Air Chief Marshal, graduate and Directing Staff of the Royal Air Force Staff College, Directing Staff of the Imperial Defence College, renowned planner and thinker, and beloved and respected father of mine, what was your Aim in all this? We should be able to find the answer somewhere at the end of his Introduction.

"To bring a smile or two to the lips of my immediate progeny and of my grandchildren," is a very poor Aim. Two out of ten it would have scored on a Staff College course and the instructors' blue pencils would have been busy. So are we to conclude that his mental processes were so disorganized that he wrote all this down with no Aim in mind and produced the progeny-smiling-lips suggestion almost as an afterthought in an attempt to find an excuse for the whole undertaking; or perhaps there was an Aim that he could never quite bring himself to set down in black and white? Did he want someone to read what he had written and come to an unprompted conclusion?

I believe I understand what he had in mind. He wanted to tell the story of his generation — to mine. After retirement he was a typical member of the postwar Establishment and he shared most of this rather maligned group's conventions, morality, philosophy and politics. These were outlined in *The Musings*. Then, because he always believed that Experience Makes the Man, he determined to record the experiences that forged his own remarkable character: *The Memories*. He had no axe to grind; he didn't need honour or recognition; he sought no thanks or public appreciation. He simply wanted people to know what it was like to live in those wonderful, exciting and tragic years that spanned two world wars and the death of an Empire; times when only those with the sharpest wits and the greatest skills could survive and yet wit and skill were no protection against the random bullet or the accident of disease. To survive, men of that generation needed good fortune or their God's protection. My father knew, I am sure, that there were many occasions when only the intervention of an inexplicably benign Fate engineered his survival. The anecdotes are his way of saying 'thankyou' although in his more introspective moments one can tell that he is not quite sure to whom his thanks should be conveyed.

'Chaps', his nickname, was not an outstanding man, merely a typical member of an outstanding generation of men — the Edwardian Military Gentlemen, who, with a loyalty that nowadays is almost impossible to comprehend, supported God, the Monarch and the Empire during the first 70 years of this century and loved every marvellous, adventurous minute of it.

To go back to the introduction, I feel that it was my father's Aim to get me to read and digest the journals and archives. The smile that he was hoping to bring to my lips was one of understanding, not of mirth. In the same way as I respected him for his experience and success, he looked to me for my youth and my energy. At the age of thirty I could do many of the things that he once excelled at. I could fly a jet fighter and pick out a tune on the piano; I could chat to pretty girls at parties and where I led people sometimes followed; but most of all I could write a bit and I feel that this is the message of the journals.

"See if some day you can string my stuff together, son. You knew me;
you know what I want to say. Tell 'em what it was like; tell 'em what
I was like; and, above all, tell 'em what fun it all was."

Between us he hoped that we could write a sympathetic history of his generation which would explain to readers what it was that made these grand old men tick. He wanted people to know how wide of the mark they were when they thought of his generation as conceited, conservative and pig-headed. How admirable was their loyalty; how absolute their love of freedom and how enviable their certainty that what they believed in and fought for was absolutely, cast-iron, copper-bottomed, question-if-you-dare right.

So this is my introduction.

My father was under no illusions about the significance of his life as an individual long-serving and fairly senior military officer. He realized that his career fell short of the international importance that makes biographies readable for factual content alone. He wasn't present at the signing of any surrenders, nor did he have the ear of any great military commanders in the wars. The significance of his life lies in the ordinary rather than the dramatic. He realized that he had lived and survived in exciting times and that the role he played in the first 60 years of this century from fledgling pilot in the RFC to Vice Chief of Air Staff was a role that never again would be on offer to the young men of this country. He understood that his ideas and morals and the likes and dislikes about which he felt so strongly were fashioned by the many adventures of his life. He wanted to tell the story of his generation and to rebut the notion that only the youth of today know how to live. He needed to explain his pleasures and apologize for his mistakes. My Aim, therefore, is to bring to life my father's notebooks and to tell his story as he would have it told.

CHAPTER ONE

CHILDHOOD AND SCHOOLDAYS

"A different sort of bravery, of a more old-fashioned kind... was displayed by a senior officer in the RAF with unexpected consequences. (Sir) Ronald Ivelaw-Chapman came from what in the Hapsburg monarchy used to be called a *Kaderfamilie* – that is, he belonged to the old officer class."

(*M I 9 Escape and Evasion*, Foot and Langley, 1979.)

In fact nothing could be further from the truth than this casual and clearly unresearched classification of the Ivelaw-Chapman background.

In reality my father's father was a merchant adventurer of Franco-Jewish extraction and his mother the mixed-race offspring of a Scotsman and a French Creole. Far from being of the officer class, Joseph Chapman was a triumphantly self-made merchant in the white-man's-grave colony of British Guiana where, as a young man, he swept the floors in Georgetown's only general store and twenty years later owned the company.

Joseph was one of eight brothers, and for many years a large proportion of the expatriate population of British Guiana shared the surname Chapman. To counter the annoyance of being presented with his relatives' unpaid bills, the newly prosperous merchant sought a prefix for his surname. He chose an anglicized version of the name of a close friend, Captain Ivalov, who commanded a Russian cargo ship. The Captain regularly transported cargo from Russia to British Guiana, much of which ended up on the shelves of Joseph Chapman's increasingly successful store. The two men did business in the Captain's cabin, and over several years and many glasses of vodka they became firm friends. When the captain died unexpectedly in an accident their friendship was commemorated in the first part of the Ivelaw-Chapman surname.

The name may sound grand, even aristocratic, but, like the modest family fortune and the middle-class respectability that it bought, it was all a product of Joseph Chapman's unrelenting industry in the unfriendly climate of Georgetown, British Guiana, during the last fifteen years of the Queen Empress's reign.

Young Ronald was four years old when his parents brought him back to England in 1903. At this time, when the British Empire was at its most successful and powerful, there were plenty like the Ivelaw-Chapman family making a new home in the old country after a rewarding career in the colonies. They were mostly unsettled people who found it hard to put down roots and find a place in the rigid pecking order of Edwardian society. They had money – hard earned, not inherited – and experience; they could deal with natives and servants but found it hard to make friends in England. They invested wisely and bought elegant homes. They paid for the best schooling for their offspring, but somehow they never quite integrated and were largely unsuccessful in their almost fanatical search for respectability. The marriage of Joseph Ivelaw-Chapman and his wife Shirley was by all accounts stormy. Like so many successful entrepreneurs, he was a difficult husband but a devoted father. Not generous with his money, he nevertheless tried to provide the best for his family from whom he was separated for most of each year between 1900 and 1920. He regularly returned to Georgetown to supervise the running of the department store, and was apparently relieved to get away, having settled his wife in various elegant homes and his children in impeccable educational establishments. The Biographical Notes make a cursory reference to his childhood and school days.

In 1906 I was sent to the Junior School of Cheltenham College at the age of 7, first as a day boy and later – much to my delight – as a boarder. Nothing particular stands out in my memory of the 7 years I spent at the Junior save for the great respect and admiration it engendered in me for its bachelor headmaster; C.I. Thornton esq. During my last term there I was made head boy of the school and learnt some of the advantages of being given responsibility at a very early age. I was no real scholar but I managed to get by in most subjects and found Latin particularly to my taste. At the end of my time in the Junior I was made to sit the scholarship exam for the Senior, but I was not successful. My time in the Senior (Cheltenham College proper) spread from 1913 to 1917 and thus was highly coloured by war and its effects on our national life. At College, as in nearly every other section of my life, I excelled at nothing. I soon discovered that I wasn't very good at cricket and turned over to rowing at which I was nothing more than passable. I enjoyed rugger but never qualified for anything more distinguished than my House first fifteen.

I did have a natural bent for swimming and in my last summer I won the 17 lengths in the College baths and also the Half Mile swum in the Severn at Tewkesbury. Academically I achieved little, spending most of my years in the Lower VIth Classical. The form master was Graeme Patterson who taught me a lot about life and whose philosophy still clings to me today. He and I were friends for years after I left College. I never reached the dizzy heights of Upper VIth Classical nor showed any real promise as a scholar.

If we are considering the complex character of the Edwardian Military Gentleman as exemplified in Ronald Ivelaw-Chapman we should examine in more depth what he actually learnt in the public school environment and more particularly what he absorbed from the two masters that he chose to mention by name fifty years after he graduated from Cheltenham College.

By the age of nine he was a boarder at Cheltenham prep-school and there is no reason to doubt that he loved it. The idea that it is good for the character to take a nine-year-old boy away from home and thrust him into the harsh regime of a British prep-school for two-thirds of each year has gradually lost favour with educationalists. The system made some boys but it undoubtedly broke others. Perhaps in his case young Ronald appreciated the security that the school gave him in contrast to the rather unsettled nature of his home life. What is surprising is that he was sufficiently introspective, even at such an early age, to appreciate the good it was doing him. As a father and as a grandfather he provided for the private education for his progeny, but with the strict proviso that the boys should go to boarding school.

"The great lessons of school," he would say, "are not learned in the classroom but in the corridors, studies and dormitories, where a boy learns how to live with his fellows."

Learning to live with his fellows meant an understanding of the importance of manners, of tolerance, of compliance with the accepted order of things; add to this an exaggerated unselfishness and a sense of duty to the community and we can get an idea of the regime that was so successfully overseen by Messrs C.I. Thornton esq, Graeme Patterson *et al.*

What is unusual in what would otherwise be a rather straightforward analysis of the benefits of education in the early 20th century British public school system is that young Ronald Ivelaw-Chapman never questioned the values drummed into him. While at Cheltenham College he never asked, "What is the point of learning Latin?" any more than he questioned the school's authority to force him into the O.T.C and at the age of twelve to teach him how to drill with rifle and bayonet and shoot holes in targets that looked like Germans on the range at Seven Springs. And for the rest of his life until his retirement as Chairman of the Board of Governors of Cheltenham College in the early 1970s, he never had any doubts that manners, tolerance, compliance with the accepted order of things, unselfishness and a sense of duty were the tenets that made a British Public School education simply the best that there was.

And who can say that he wasn't right? The playing fields of Eton were supposed to have engendered the great victory at Waterloo and in the same way the rugger pitches, studies and dormitories of our minor public schools produced the military officers and colonial administrators who saw us successfully through two World Wars and administered with skill and impartiality the far-flung operation of the British Empire. In the view of the Edwardian Military Gentleman there can be no greater success story.

There is one other important characteristic that he seems to have learnt at Cheltenham; an awesome self-discipline. From a very early age he had the ability to oversee and control his behaviour from within. "Make it your servant not your master," he would say about almost any indulgence, from tobacco to gambling, from driving too fast to collecting stamps. "Only the unintelligent get bored," was another catch-phrase he used proudly to indicate that he had the power to force his brain to work fully even in times of physical inactivity, and from this sprang a remarkable mental endurance which enabled him to tolerate pain and loneliness at various times in his life and to fill every moment of his consciousness with rewarding activity.

He was of course instructed in the Anglican faith at school and once again there seems to be no sign that he ever questioned the dogma of Protestant religion. For most of his life Christianity was merely a discipline; part of the duty of service which was so important to him and also part of the accepted order of things which he never considered opposing. From a very early age the rules by which he governed his life were his own and owed more to Humanism than to the Ten Commandments.

In a section headed Pre-1918 Memories, the Biographical Notes tell us how young Ron, as the family knew him, spent extremely happy holidays away from school.

My more vivid recollections of these formative years stem mainly from holidays as opposed to termtime. During most of this period we lived in a largish house, (Treweeth) perched high above the Cornish fishing village of St Ives. Father had acquired a Sunbeam open tourer of, I think, 1916 vintage. It was a lovely motor car which I was occasionally allowed to drive. With its help we and our friends explored the whole of the north and south coasts of Cornwall, from Bude round Land's End to St Mawes on the Fal. We picnicked, swam, rock-climbed, sunbathed and thoroughly enjoyed ourselves in some of the prettiest and least-known coves and bays in Cornwall. My affection for that part of England has stayed with me all my life and I remember when I was in Solitary Confinement during the 1939-45 war I used to go in my mind systematically all round the coast of West Cornwall trying to recall the approach to, and special attraction of, each of the coves. Such names still linger in my memory; Pedn y Vounder and Rinsey; Gunwalloe and St Ruan Minor; Zennor and the charmingly named St Just in Roseland.

One year when I was still at school, 1916 I think, I had just acquired a 2¾hp Douglas motorbike. I was old enough to have a licence and about a week before Christmas I set off from Cheltenham on this little device for the 250-mile trip to St Ives. Not all the details of that eventful journey remain with me but I do remember driving some 20 miles or so across Bodmin Moor in a snowstorm with only a flickering acetylene headlamp and no goggles. I remember too the corner of my Burberry Mackintosh (my only protection against the weather) getting caught in the chain cog of the fly wheel which set me back quite a lot in time and effort. I also vividly remember the expression of relief on Mother's face when eventually I showed up at our house in St Ives well after 2 am on a bitter winter's night some 10 hours later than I was expected.

This then is what we know of Ronald Ivelaw-Chapman as he comes to the end of his schooling and embarks gleefully, like millions of his doomed contemporaries, on the murderous adventure of the First World War. He was moderately educated and able to stand on his own feet; he was devoted to his mother but anxious to break out of the family's grasp. He was Christian, loved mechanical things and was motor-bike mad, but he also appreciated beautiful scenery and wild landscapes. He was courageous, healthy and already keen to pit his strength against physical discomfort. His duty was simple and clear. Without a moment's hesitation and at the earliest possible moment he stepped forward to serve his king and country. The date was 17 January, 1918.

CHAPTER TWO

TRAINING FOR WAR IN THE AIR

The Biographical Notes record Cadet Ivelaw-Chapman's early days in the Royal Flying Corps.

When I was still at school and aged 17 I enlisted in "Kitchener's Army" which entitled me to wear a khaki armband with my civilian clothes. Such was the misplaced patriotism in 1916 that many women walked the streets distributing white feathers to any young lad whom they considered to be of military age but not in uniform. These "K" armbands were partly a protection against such indignity and partly a token of commitment to enlist on one's 18th birthday. This I did, leaving Cheltenham College in the morning and being enlisted in the R.F.C. as a third class air mechanic during the same afternoon at Farnborough. Soon after, I became an Officer Cadet and was allowed to wear a white hatband on my "Fore and Aft" R.F.C. hat. About 6 weeks later, or as early as was permissible, I applied for a 48-hour weekend pass with the idea of visiting my family to show off my uniform. As a matter of routine, before you could get your pass signed you had to go before a Medical Officer to have it stamped "FFI" (Fit and Free from Infection). This MO took one look at my chest, tore up the pass and ordered me to report to the isolation ward of the local sickbay as a chicken pox (or was it a measles?) case. He was right and I was soon in bed in a stuffy little ward with about 20 beds in it. I didn't feel particularly ill at the time but I was running a bit of a temperature. That night the soldier in the next bed to me died in great agony with his knees drawn almost up to his chin. His death was due to cerebro-spinal meningitis, or more commonly "Spotted Fever", and there was no small amount of panic the next morning. All the patients in the wards had swabs taken from the backs of their throats from which it was discovered that at least four of us were carriers of this dread disease. So off I was packed to the main Aldershot Isolation Hospital in some remote spot well outside the town and there I remained for the next three months. I was the only cadet in a soldiers' ward and found it all pretty tough going after my sheltered life at home and at school. However, it did me a lot of good and I learnt a bit about the workings of the ordinary Tommy's mind. My greatest enemy was boredom — I was too young then to have learnt how to counter that — because our only treatment was being fumigated for ten minutes a day in a small hermetically sealed hut. Apart from that there was nothing to do and no exercise. Eventually the day came for my release and I went back to cadet camp at Farnborough where I found that all my friends had moved up to the next stage of their training. I, too, soon moved on and there followed a drill and discipline course at Oxford (I was billeted in Corpus Christi) where our instructors were ex-Guards Sergeant Majors and we were put through the "Square Bashing" business in a big way, a schooling I have never regretted. Currently with that we had classes in Morse Code, map reading, internal combustion engine, theory of flight etc.

He was actually presented with a white feather during one of his school holidays in St Ives in 1916. The fact that he could only bring himself to mention this 60 years later and, only in general terms, when writing about the benefits of joining Kitchener's Army, indicates the immense psychological impact this incident must have had on him. He was so far removed from being a coward that he admitted going down on his knees while at school and praying to God that the First World War would last long enough for him to be able to take part in it. He describes as "Misplaced Patriotism" the motives of women who took it upon themselves to accuse young men, barely of military age, of cowardice in this particularly public and unpleasant way. Most survivors of the First World War would have had a rather more jaundiced opinion of the women who bullied and cajoled them into volunteering for service at the front.

The meningitis incident must be recorded as one of the remarkably fortunate incidents in his life. Not only did fate permit him to contract this virtually incurable disease only as a carrier, but the three-month delay caused in his training meant that he arrived on active service that much nearer the end of the War. Most of the friends who "had moved up to the next stage of their training" did not survive the period at the end of 1917 when the Royal Flying Corps suffered very heavy casualties in France. Throughout his life he used the word "tough" as in "I found it all pretty tough going" as a description, almost a euphemism, for "of lower class". Here is the officer cadet unceremoniously placed in the great social melting pot of a hospital isolation ward and it was probably the only time in his life that he woke up with a private soldier in the next bed. His assertion that it "did him a lot of good" is true. He had gone straight from public school into an Army that was feudal in its class structure. If it hadn't been for these three months at Aldershot he probably would have passed the next 30 years of his life without ever holding a conversation with someone who wasn't of "commissioned status". The Edwardian Military claimed to be uninfluenced by class in the selection of their friends and confidants; they would argue fiercely that the commission system in the Armed Forces was based on merit rather than social status. But snobs they were, to the largest extent in the matter of recruitment, where it was possible to ensure that only "our sort of people" survived the selection boards for officer training establishments. The close-knit society of officers' mess and military club ensured that officers rarely looked outside their own particular circle for social contact. Chaps was a little different. He never committed the great military folly of imagining that a man's intelligence was commensurate with his rank. His closest and most enduring Second World War friendship was with the Australian sergeant who was shot down with him in 1944. In retirement he loved to talk, over the garden wall, to the smallholders and tenant farmers who were his neighbours; putting the world to rights over a beer or a glass of port.

Biographical Notes. Early Days in the R.F.C.

Then the great day came when I was posted to No 12 F.T.S [Flying Training School] at Thetford and I saw an aeroplane at close quarters for the first time. The aeroplane was the Maurice Farman Shorthorn, very much of the "Sticks and String" type, where one sat far out into the nose with no face shield and was pushed through the air by a 70hp engine and propeller. I was in the air on "Dual" the same afternoon of my arrival and I see from my logbook that after 5¼ hours of dual I was let loose in the sky by myself — and was I happy! The next stage came at No 53 F.T.S Narborough and later at Harlaxton where after some 50 mins of dual I was given a D.H.6 to fly. This rugged, graceless but cheap de Havilland product was known — I can't think why — as the "Clutching Hand". But I found its qualities quite belied its looks and I got very fond of it during the 21-odd hours I put in flying it. Possibly its attraction lay in the fact that I found I could loop the loop in it quite easily and do other forms of mild aerobatics. On Jan. 11th 1918 I qualified for my Wings on the R.E.8, a machine that had at the time a rather unsavoury reputation for killing a lot of its pilots. However, I managed to get in some 7 hours of solo on it and remained unscathed. In February of 1918 I was sent down to Worthy Down near Winchester to be converted on to the Armstrong Whitworth with the 160hp Beardmore engine, commonly known as the Big Ack. I see, again from my log book, that during my week at Worthy Down I managed to get in 10 minutes' dual and just over 7 hours solo on the Big Ack. Shortly afterwards I left to join my first Active Service Squadron in France.

One of the more pleasant sides of being in the Royal Flying Corps in those days was the elegant uniform that we wore. We were dressed in the so-called Maternity Jacket, a double-breasted affair which we wore with smart breeches and field boots. To my mind it was the most distinguished uniform ever designed for military service. But apart from its smartness it had an in-built convenience. When one was on early flying, which often started at dawn, the whole outfit could be slipped over one's pyjamas; long waist-high "Fug boots" replacing the field boots. The R.F.C was considered a Corps d'Elite during that war; far more so, I think, than the R.A.F. in Hitler's War. But whether that was so or not we felt terribly pleased to be in it, particularly after we had graduated and could wear the much prized R.F.C. Wings on our tunics.

Carefully bound and annotated among the archives were a series of handwritten letters that Ronald wrote to his mother during his early days as a pilot. They are evocative and poignant in language and content. This one is dated 29 October, 1917.

Royal Flying Corps
Thetford
Norfolk

My Dearest Mater,
   Just a line to thank you for yours and notebook.
Perhaps you'll be glad and perhaps you will not to hear that I've started my solo. In fact I've put in 25 mins. I did my first on Saturday; a sublime day, not the slightest breath of wind or a single bump. I did a circuit and then made a perfect landing. My instructor was very pleased indeed. On Monday morning I went up and put in 20 mins and 2 landings. In the second I made a bad landing but the only damage was a couple of wires in the undercarriage broken. As soon as I have finished my four hours solo I hope to get leave. This may be tomorrow and it may be two months hence. We are simply crowded out. More pupils than the instructors can possibly deal with owing to the dud weather. I had a splendid game of Rugger against the Command Depot R.E.s today. Of course we won. There's another game on Friday. By Jove we do want some exercise here; as flying is a very relaxing sort of game. (That's what it is; it is only a game.) Give my love to all concerned

Yours, Ron.

A first solo in a flying machine ranks alongside a miner's first nervous descent of a coalmine shaft as a definitive moment of demarcation between boyhood and manhood. Most people who have lived through a first solo will say that it is one of life's great experiences. You are awesomely alone; no advice from experience; no encouragement; no reminders; no going back. Flyers grow immeasurably in spirit and confidence after their first solos; drinks are bought, mementos exchanged and for a short while the instructor who has watched it all happen from the ground is accorded the status of a God. Cadet Chapman transmits little of the magnitude of the moment in this rather boyish letter to his mother, but we should not be misled. He is rejoicing. There is significance too in the choice of the word sublime; it is quite unexpected in a letter where the language is far more conversational: "dud weather... splendid game of rugger... By Jove we do want some exercise." Sublime is more a Songs of Praise word, or maybe Gilbert and Sullivan. Perhaps we can imagine that even on his first solo, with goggles down and scarf blowing in the wind, with all his utmost concentration engaged in manipulating the rpm, adjusting height and speed, and making allowance for wind and drift, Cadet Chapman was sufficiently captivated with the romance and beauty of flight to note that on 26 October, 1917, at Thetford in Norfolk the day and the weather and the view from a lonely machine at one thousand feet were sublime.

The next two letters are devoted largely to telling his mother about his first crash and then endeavouring to persuade her not to worry about it.

No 53 Training Squadron
Harlaxton
Lincs.

My Dear Mother,
Please excuse pencil as I am writing this in bed at 11pm. I have had the most exciting day. In fact I've had my first crash (no one hurt) on that foolproof bus, a D H 6. It happened like this. I asked my instructor if I could take a bus up this morning and he said I had done so long on the D H 6 he would come up with me, sit in the front and give me some forced landings. I took him round for about ¼ hour, then he took control and started looking down for fields; all of a sudden he throttled back his engine and shouted to me to land the bus.... I spotted what looked a nice field, spiralled down but overshot it and all of a sudden found we were running into a huge great tree. I tried to zoom up over it but my engine wouldn't take it so my instructor avoided the tree by making a vertical bank and side slipped on to the ground, hitting it with our left wing first. She went up on her nose and stuck there. All we did was to climb down out of the machine. The damage was two bottom planes, an undercarriage, one or two struts and a prop.... It is a most extraordinary thing but I have just realized I've cost the government just about £500 today. Oh how I wish I had it in cash. I must go to sleep now,

So cheerioh and good night
Ron.

Harlaxton
Wednesday
Evening
Dec 1917

My Darling Mother
    First of all please excuse dirty paper and accept acknowledgement of 2
letters from you received on Monday and 1 from Eileen received tonight;
also 1 pump, 1 packet of buttons and 1 bicycle with bell complete. Now,
to business. I don't want you to get upset about that crash of mine, because
minor things like that are of every-day occurrence at an aerodrome. I have
been extraordinarily lucky not to have had a dozen or more similar ones in
the 32 hours I have put in the air. In fact only yesterday a fellow went up
in a machine and his engine cut out just above a wood and he landed in a
tree with bits of branches sticking through the planes in all directions. The
machine stuck up there and it was quite a time before the pilot could get
down. Eventually he climbed down the tree and needless to say he wasn't
hurt in the slightest. You can be well assured my nerve has not been impaired
in the slightest by standing a D H 6 on its nose. Constant rumours are going
round as to Xmas leave but everything is in the melting pot at present; but
set your mind to spending Xmas without your son and heir. I'm afraid it is
out of the question for you to come up here as there are only two hotels in
Grantham worthy of the name and I wouldn't like to see you quartered in
either. Yes, I expect to finish on R E 8s which at present is the service bus
for art. obs., but by the time I get out there it will probably be the Bristol
Fighter; the finest machine in the air of its type fitted with a 250 Rolls
Engine and a large margin of stability, no extensions, an adjustable
tailplane and a faster machine. In fact Art Obs on a B.F. will be one of
the safest jobs in France... so there is nothing to be alarmed about. Please
put sew-on buttons on the other shirts. The collar band was quite OK. As
regards an Xmas present my taste is somewhat extravagant; these are a few
suggestions. A flying helmet; a pair of flying goggles; an identification disc;
a shaving mirror or any other usable articles. Above all please don't get me
anything ornamental.

Most of this is a classic "Don't worry Mum, I'll be all right" serviceman's
letter. If a soldier is to go to war with high morale, he must be convinced
during his training that he is all but invincible. Battle-scarred instructors
tell recruits that their army is the best, their equipment the most efficient

and their armour so strong that the enemy has no hope of piercing it. They are also usually told that God is on their side and that generations as yet unborn will never be able to thank sufficiently the young men who are preparing to go off and fight in the cause of justice and civilization. Recruits believe all this because recruits believe everything, and in their letters home they try and pass on their optimism. It is rather sad because it is clear that Mum needs a lot more convincing of her son's invulnerability than the young man does himself. Cadet Chapman's mother wouldn't have been comforted at all by the fact that the Bristol Fighter had "a large margin of stability, no extensions and an adjustable tailplane". The hour of her son's posting to the war in France was approaching and she knew that once over there only God's own luck would protect him. People who have been to boarding school or done military service will recognize a reluctance on the part of young men to introduce their parents, more particularly their mothers, into these worlds. Mrs Ivelaw-Chapman was being hustled out of the idea of visiting her son at Harlaxton. There were in fact two excellent coaching hotels in Grantham. One of them, The Angel and Royal has a historical reputation for comfort and hospitality to travellers on the Great North Road. It was certainly grand enough for the ex-colonial Ivelaw-Chapmans and she would have been aware of it. But she must have understood his reluctance to let her visit him because, after this gentle brush-off, she never again proposed it.

The Christmas present list is significant. He may have thought his selection extravagant but how austere it looks today. Helmets, goggles and identity discs were in fact Service issue to trainee pilots. A preoccupation with shaving with soap, mirror and razor was typical of this generation. They were fastidious men who even in old age didn't like to face a new day unclean or unshaven. In the armed forces of the Crown shaving equated with normality and if an Edwardian Military Gentleman woke up in a foxhole or a prison cell or in a tented mess in the desert his first compelling instinct was to send for soap, water and the razor. Applying the same principle that bodily functions were somehow slightly insulting to one's near neighbours, these men would excuse themselves in company before blowing their noses or mopping their brows. They never considered using what are known today as toiletries and, while a shaving mirror was an acceptable gift for a young airman about to embark for active service in the First World War, a bottle of Old Spice would have gone straight down the drain.

Letter to his Mother. December, 1917, continued.

Yes, my Instructor Jackson is only a Second Lieutenant. Now I must tell you of 3 hrs 20 mins that I did in the air today. My Flight Commander told me I was to go on my cross country flight test in a D H 6. Two others started also but one lost his way and had to make a forced landing. We had to report at the aerodrome at South Carlton about 5 miles north (the far side) of Lincoln and at Spittlegate (Wing HQ) about 3 miles away just outside Grantham. I took the lead and followed the railway line up to Lincoln flying over an R.N.A.S. Aerodrome at Cranwell and also Waddington (Freddie's Squadron). From Lincoln I could see South Carlton. I landed there — made a top hole landing — reported and flew back with the other fellow just behind me as far as Grantham where for some unknown reason he left me and lost his way and was not heard of till late tonight. He also had a forced landing. I landed at Spittlegate and reported to the Wing and returned to base just in time for lunch at 1. I was in the air for 2 hrs and 40 mins and enjoyed it tremendously. The ground was a mass of white; it was quite calm and brilliant sunshine. I was flying at 3,000 feet and could see for miles and miles. I could see the Great North Road stretching ahead for miles. There was a ground mist over Lincoln and I came down to about 1500 feet and seemed to be about 50 feet above the cathedral spire but in reality I was more like 1200 feet above it. It was beautifully clear and I traced my whole course on the map as I went along (one hand on the joy-stick and one holding the map). I had a splendid engine which gave me full revs the whole way and did not miss once. In fact the conditions were ideal. Of the three that started I was the only one to make a success of it, but why the others didn't I can't understand as the course was as simple as ABC.

After the adventure of this first navigation trip Chaps was never known to throw a map away. Wherever he happened to be residing throughout his career there was always a desk and at least half the desk's capacity was given over to maps. During the Second World War when civilians were instructed to destroy maps in case they were of assistance to the enemy after invasion, part of his hoard was solemnly and disobediently hidden under the floorboards of the house in Cheltenham. If in later years some one asked him the best route, say, from Spittlegate to South Carlton, he could be relied upon to find a map of the area, hopelessly out of date, but with the track of a long forgotten navex still traced on it and a faint cross in pencil that showed where once he had fixed his position.

This letter is probably the earliest example of an aviator's mystical affinity with Lincoln Cathedral. "There is only one hill in Lincolnshire," a flying man will tell you, "and that's got a dirty great church on the top." But fliers will also tell of how this glorious building acted as a guide, perhaps even a beacon of hope to frightened men in flying machines straining their eyes for a familiar feature in an unresponsive flatland. Lancasters and Wellingtons inbound to Scampton and Waddington; Flight Cadets in Balliols and Jet Provosts desperately searching for Cranwell; Students in Vampires night-flying from Swinderby, Wigsley, Winthorpe, Skellingthorpe, Woodhall Spa. So many men have relaxed and felt themselves a little safer when Lincoln Cathedral came into view that some say the building had about it a visible aura of welcome. Strange to note that R I-C comments to his mother on the "Cathedral Spire at Lincoln". The building in fact doesn't have a spire; it has twin towers. Could all this eulogy about Lincoln be a dreadful mistake? Was he perhaps over Newark on Trent all the time?

In February 1918 Second Lieutenant R. Ivelaw-Chapman, R.F.C. went to War.

CHAPTER 3

THE FIRST WORLD WAR

The Biographical Notes give a brief description of what he remembered, in the early 1970s, of life on a Royal Flying Corps Squadron in early 1918.

My recollections of those exciting 11 months that I spent with No 10 Squadron are a curious mixture and quite understandably so. For here I was, just turned nineteen, having learned to fly 'on a shoestring' as it were, suddenly pitchforked into battle in the middle of a devastating war. The first thing that was brought home to me when I joined the squadron at Abeele on the Franco-Belgian border was my relative immaturity. Not only was I much younger than most of the other pilots and observers in the squadron but I was far less experienced in worldly matters. I had come from the protective shelter of public school life straight into the R.F.C. and now, only a few months later I found myself a qualified pilot with considerable responsibility and on active service. How I got away with it I just can't imagine, but of course the main stimulus was the excitement and novelty of it all. In my early days at Abeele I was at pains to keep my ears and eyes open and my mouth firmly closed. By this means I soon learned which of my fellow pilots I could take as the standard for me to aim at, and this seemed to work all right. A great surprise came about half way through my tour with the squadron. Major Keith Murray, my revered CO, offered me command of B Flight with the acting rank of Captain (We were still R.F.C.) at the age of 19. This gave me a tremendous moral boost. Shortly afterwards I was one of only three pilots chosen to fly the Bristol Fighter which had been sent out for us to try out for the sort of flying we were engaged upon.

Our work in No 10 Squadron was mainly that of Artillery Observation; not particularly exacting work nor as glamorous as that of the Scout Squadrons, but quite exciting enough for me. We usually worked with a battery of field artillery and flew more or less over the battery's target behind the German lines and reported back to the battery by wireless the exact fall of their shells using a simple Clock Code. On other occasions we were on Contact Patrol. During the rare periods of open warfare we worked with the infantry and by dropping messages in streamlined message bags we told them the type of opposition or terrain they were next likely to encounter.

*We also did quite a lot of photographic work on the German side of the front
line to help our intelligence. The disadvantage of this type of work was that
we were flying a relatively slow aeroplane and always fairly low down.
Thus we were quite an attractive target for the much faster German Scouts
who used to dive down on their prey with the sun behind them. We carried
an Observer with a Lewis gun and it was his job to see that we were not
caught out whilst we, the pilots, were busy watching the ground and spotting
the fall of shells for our gunner friends.*

This condensed and uninspiring report is all that was recorded in the
Biographical Notes that cover the First World War. However, the letters,
mainly to his mother, that he wrote from the Front in Belgium give a more
revealing description of a great military experience. The first letter is
datelined BEF Feb 1918, just days after he joined Number 10 Squadron.

My Darling Mother,
   *Many thanks for yours addressed to 2 AS O (Without enclosure!) Well I
think I have struck oil this time. I arrived at this squadron on Saturday
night and was posted to C Flight. Each Flight has a different Mess
consisting of about 20 Officers. C Flight is the Headquarters Flight and the
CO and Ground Officers mess with us so you can imagine we do ourselves
pretty well. We invariably have a four course and generally a five or six
course dinner in the evenings; soup, fish, meat, sweets, savoury and dessert.
At lunch we get a course of at least 6 dishes; lobster mayonnaise, cottage
pie, cold brawn, hash, meat etc.etc. The ante room, though small is very
comfortable and includes a piano, gramophone and all the latest periodicals
and magazines. The daily papers (All) we get just one day late. The sleeping
quarters are little huts, 2 in each, very nicely got up (with a stove) and very
cosy. On the day after I arrived I played rugger for the Squadron against
another Squadron and managed to beat them 21 nil. It was quite a good
game. That night I was invited over to mess with A Flight and spent a
very jolly evening. My Flight Commander is a tip-top fellow and a first-
rate pilot. He is quite young and a mixture between Capt. Harrison of
Thetford and Jackson. First of all he took me round and showed me the
'drome and then I took a machine up myself and satisfied him. Yesterday
one of the old Observers took me up and showed me the Line and I had
my first dose of Archie which needless to say was miles wide. The Observer
fired a few rounds into Hunland and I leave it to you to draw your
conclusions. It may interest you to know, if our friend the Censor will let
you, that I saw the ruins of Ypres from 7000 ft; a very weird spectacle.
   The Squadron is just a quiet little colony and quite peaceful; one might
just as well be in England. This morning I was to have done my first job:*

the 'Early Show', in other words the dawn patrol. However, the weather was absolutely dud; all aviation being prevented by a very low mist. I really must stop now. Oh, I am enclosing a cheque for 16/- which please send to Messrs Wright and tell them to send me out 200 Grand Format cigarettes. Also tell Plants to send me out some R.F.C. pocket (Small) buttons for my tunics and two pairs of stockings. (I think they are called woollen knee hose?) Tell Mr Tyler I want them big and of a quiet hue. I really must stop now as I have to do a practice shoot.

Lots of Love,
Ron.

"Every man thinks meanly of himself for not having been a soldier."

(Johnson)

People who have not fought in wars look with hero-worship at those who have. What was it like? How do you overcome fear? Does the proximity of death heighten your every experience? What is it like to kill a man? What is it like to be wounded? What is it like to die? Those who have never been soldiers have all the questions but rarely are they satisfactorily answered.

At first glance Lieutenant Ivelaw-Chapman in his letter to his mother and, 50 years later in his Service Memories, answers none of the familiar questions about war. He tells his readers that the Bristol Fighter was a lovely aeroplane and that 'Art Obs.' Armstrong Whitworth Big Acks were an attractive target for the German Scouts. We learn that lobster mayonnaise was on the lunch menu in some RFC Messes and that 200 hand-rolled cigarettes were quite an important feature in the life of an intrepid young flying man. But did his hand ever shake? Did he get nightmares? If his observer fired a few rounds into Hunland did men and horses actually fall over? That first dose of 'Archie'; of course it was miles wide; Anti-Aircraft fire apparently always is unless it hits you, but was his reaction to run away from it in fear or simply to disregard the pretty but lethal puffs of smoke and shrapnel in the sky?

No, he wasn't frightened. Certainly he would never have admitted fear in a letter to his mother, but in 1969 the mature man who freely expressed his inner thoughts on paper would have acknowledged terror if terror there had been.

He was not fearless out of stupidity. He was fearless as the young usually are in all walks of life. Be it riding a motorbike in a snow storm or swimming a little further out in the bay than is prudent; skiing down the steepest slope or flying a Big Ack within range of the German 'Archie', the young will press on without the inhibiting fear that makes older men turn back.

Other things frighten pilots. They understand that they are privileged to operate sophisticated machines in a totally unnatural environment and most pilots take tremendous pleasure in it; but only occasionally can they fly just for fun. More often they are operating for the benefit of others who are earthbound. A pilot's constant fear is that his mastery of the machine and the environment will be found wanting; that through incompetence he will let down those who have trained him, and fail in his responsibilities to those who depend on his uncommon skills. Thus a flying instructor will be most frightened when his student is in the air on his first solo; worrying that the lad will not get down again safely because some vital lesson has not been properly taught; an airline pilot will quite genuinely declare that nothing in the course of a scheduled flight causes him any fear at all except the possibility of causing death or injury to his passengers by reason of his own incompetence.

Lt Ivelaw-Chapman, newly arrived on No 10 Squadron RFC, would have been frightened to death when his Flight Commander checked him out on his first flight from the aerodrome at Abeele. Would he be good enough to be accepted into the Squadron? Would he make a hash of his first landing and have to be sent back to England for further training? The relief when it all went well can be sensed from the letter: "I took a machine up myself and satisfied him." After the testing time of his early examination by the Flight Commander, the fear generated by crossing the German lines for the first time and spotting a distant Anti-Aircraft shell burst was not worth considering.

In later years he was an acknowledged crossword fanatic and his mind was always full of clues, solutions and definitions, even when he wasn't actually solving a puzzle. We can be sure that his use of the word "weird" to describe the spectacle of the shattered township of Ypres was carefully thought out. The definition of "weird" has shifted considerably since 1918. Now it has come to mean unusual, quirky or even over-the-top; then it meant ghostly or haunted. There can be few more apt one-word descriptions for a misty view from 7000 feet of a war-ravaged town where 200,000 men had died. There is just a suspicion of lyricism here, similar to the "sublime" morning over Thetford.

Letter to his mother. 1st April, 1918.

My Darling Mater,

Just a note to tell you of a pleasant interlude that took place last night. It being the 31st of March, the Doctor (Major Murray), proposed the toast of the dying RFC and made an appropriate speech. We are now in the RAF and to celebrate the occasion I opened my career in the RAF by putting in 6 hours, all but 10 minutes, in two flights. I did 3 hrs 40 mins this morning and 2 hrs 10 mins this afternoon. It consisted of two successful shoots with which the Flight Commander was very bucked, so much so that he gave me two to do tomorrow. Please thank Ive (Chaps' sister Shirley) for her pleasant letters. I received the parcel of Properts OK. There is little news and I am very, very tired after the day's work so hope you'll excuse this short note,

Lots of Love,
Ron.

Apart from recording the occasion of the actual formation of the Royal Air Force there are two points of interest in this letter.

He was still in the RAF when its 40th anniversary was celebrated in 1958. He embarked that night on an obstacle course which very few survived and yet when he wrote the letter he probably didn't permit himself to think about events even 24 hours in the future.

On one of the flights which is mentioned in the letter and with which the Flight Commander was apparently so bucked, he carried out the action for which he was awarded the Distinguished Flying Cross.

He was immensely proud of the DFC and of all his medals. Today, twelve years after his death, they are still proudly mounted and displayed like an epitaph. His will was specific as to their disposition for the next three generations. So why do we see no mention of the action or the medal in his writings? One scrap book has the scribbled signal that announces the award, but he was never known to describe to anyone the circumstances in which he won it. The reason for this reticence lay in the Edwardian Military Gentleman's obsessive distaste for conceit. An old soldier who pointed to a ribbon on his chest, took a deep breath and started to tell the story − "and I got that one for single-handedly −" was immediately assessed as not a Gentleman, not one of us, not a member of the club and probably a liar to boot. Sir Ronald took this notion even further than most of his distinguished contemporaries. Paradoxically, in the field of his personal triumphs, he verged on being conceited about his modesty.

Part of 2 letters from the Front. 1918

...you just mustn't worry about these petty crashes of mine. They are an everyday occurrence at any aerodrome in France and England. It is only part of your experience and your training as the case may be. Mistakes must occur and engines are bound to cut out now and again; for instance nearly every day some one overshoots our small aerodrome and crashes an undercarriage. One fellow had part of his engine shot away by a passing shell and landed in a shell hole somewhere. Another had one control shot away and his observer wounded in a scrap and he piled up his bus somewhere

19

without any extra injuries to himself or the Observer. I was doing a job on the Line the other day when my engine cut out through overheating and I just managed to glide into an aerodrome I knew in the district which incidentally was a French one. My Observer and I dined with the Froggies and they did us quite well. Yesterday I went up in a sidecar and flew the machine away. All these little things are bound to occur.

Do you know the type of Bus that crashed in Cheltenham College field? As regards a list of things that I want, I can think of very few except a signet ring, a pipe or a cigarette holder.

...last night I was up late after dark dropping flares over Hunland when we got shot up and a stray bullet went through the fuselage, splintered the magazine behind my back and I felt a bit hit my elbow. I was just high enough for it to have spent its force. It grazed my leather coat and did no further damage. It was nearly a Cushy Blighty. Had I been 500 feet lower I might have been home by now. Many thanks for the parcel and its contents. All was quite OK in spite of your worry about the shirts. I think that is all the news at present,

> *Lots of Love*
> *From*
> *Ron*

He's doing well, isn't he? Today we would say that Chappie, as he was known to friends on the Squadron, or Ron, as he still signed himself to his family, was living on an adrenalin high. His life seemed to be charmed and the proximity of death coloured every experience: "There's no need to worry," he wrote to his Mother, and we can be sure that he said the same to himself each night before he fell into a dreamless sleep in his hut (two beds in each, well got up with a stove and very cosy); "Crashes I walk away from; the Archie is always miles wide; the bullets are spent forces by the time they reach my machine and if any one gets hurt it's the poor bloody Observer. Night operations or the early show, Art. Obs. or just loosing off a few rounds into Hunland. Leave it to me, Flight Commander Sir; I can hack it."

His confidence was not misplaced. He came through his nine months of combat unscathed and although his five hundred odd operational hours were interspersed with numerous engine failures, aborted take-offs, hairy landings and un-instrumented ventures into mist and cloud, he never injured himself or his crewman. Others were not so fortunate.

Letter to his Mother. August 1918. Annotated in 1964, "Back from leave; Channel Flight; a little dicey."

Army Form **W. 3194.**

W 5032—105	250,000(20)	12/15	H W V (P.1548)	Forms/W. 3194/1	
18189—3?0	200,080	3/16			

Name _Ronald Inslow Chapman_   **No.**

Address   _Hazelwell_

       College Road   _Cheltenham_

Group Number _B .105_

Date of Attestation _2nd December_   191_6_ .

     The above-named man has been attested and transferred to the Army Reserve, until required for service, when he will be sent a Notice Paper, informing him as to the date, time and place at which he is to report himself. Fourteen days' notice will be given.

     N.B.—Any change of address should be immediately notified to the Recruiting Officer _Cheltenham._

Cheltenham Station.   _W A J Holmes_   Signature.

_2/12/16_ Date.   _Cpl_   Rank.

1. Kitchener's Army Attestation Card:
'When I was at school and aged 17
I enlisted in Kitchener's Army' (p.6).

2. ' … in the great social melting pot of a hospital isolation ward' (p.7).

3. Bristol Fighter landing over trees: 'I enclose one of Yours Humbly in the Bristol' (p.24).

4. 10 Squadron RFC Aerodrome, Belgium, 1918.

France

Tuesday

...I took off from Lympne in heavy mist and clouds at 2000 feet and was out of sight of land for quite 20 minutes. You could scarcely see 100 yards in front of you. I came across by compass and struck Cape Griz Nez to an inch. About half-way across my engine started overheating and vibrating badly. It began to get worse and I was just looking for a Destroyer to put it down nearby when the coast of France loomed up and I eventually got her down at the required aerodrome with the temperature at 100 degrees, (Normal Temp 70). If I had had to go another mile or two I would have had to have forced landed. I telephoned to the Squadron as soon as I landed and one of the fellows came down and flew me back and, incidentally, gave me all the news, sad and otherwise, concerning the Squadron. I now find myself, as the result of numerous changes, as one of the most senior pilots. There are an enormous number of new faces in the Mess.

"Numerous changes", of course, meant numerous casualties, though neither the military censor nor his Mother's imagined sensibilities permitted him to write the word.

The reader is still left without a genuine "exploit". The letters record his war experiences in general terms. All letters were censored and he was fearful of seeming to "Shoot a line," even when communicating with his mother. It is to an article in the old *Blackwood's Magazine* that we must turn for an original "There I was, upside down with nothing on the clock" story. In spite of its deadpan delivery the tale is genuinely hair-raising.

'Dicing with G.' *Blackwood's Magazine*; August, 1969.

On my eighteenth birthday I joined the RFC and not long afterwards found myself on a combat squadron in France flying Armstrong Whitworth two-seaters. My Observer, Lt. Fletcher, and I were on dawn patrol one morning and just before sunrise we trundled over the grass to do our three-hour stint. Half-way across the airfield the engine spluttered, checked, and then came back to full power. As a result, just before we became airborne, I struck a pile of stones on the edge of the aerodrome road. We gave a slight lurch and then gained height normally. I asked Fletcher to poke his head down through the camera hole in the floor of the machine, just behind his seat, to see what damage had been done. He reported that the undercarriage had suffered badly; it was hanging by one 'V' strut only. Beneath my seat was a rack carrying four bombs. These were supposedly 'Safe' until they were dropped, but a short time before an aeroplane belonging to another squadron had landed with bombs on the racks and they had gone off and blown the occupants to smithereens. I therefore decided to get rid of the bombs as authorized by dropping them on targets of opportunity on the German side of the line. I would then be in a much safer configuration to cope with a crash landing without wheels.

We spent the next 2 hours over the German lines where I got rid of the bombs and all our machine-gun ammunition. On the way home, with half an hour's petrol left, I ordered Fletcher to check that all the bombs had fallen clear. He gloomily reported that three of the bombs had gone but that the fourth had lodged itself securely on the dangling strut, just below me. We had no parachutes; and the bomb, having left the rack, had fused itself and was now well and truly 'Live'.

My first thought was to dunk ourselves, the bomb and the aeroplane in the North Sea which was 20 minutes' flying time away. I wrote a message to drop on my squadron headquarters telling them what I proposed to do. Then I spotted the Zillibeke Lake, five thousand feet underneath us and on our side of the lines, and this gave me an idea. The Observer had a crude form of dual control in his cockpit; I handed over to him, climbed out on the lower wing, lay flat along it and tried to reach the bomb in order to push it off the strut. The bomb proved to be out of my reach and the aeroplane went into a spin. Somehow I regained my seat and took over control. Petrol was running low and in desperation we both strapped ourselves in tightly and I flew the first half of a loop. At the top I deliberately hung upside down for about ten seconds and to my immense relief I felt a slight, dull thud on the inverted bottom of the machine. Gravity had come to our aid and dislodged the bomb. I completed the loop; the bomb fell away and we looked down at the surface of the Zillibeke Lake where the bomb exploded harmlessly a few seconds later.

On return to the aerodrome I flew low to show them that I was booked for an abrupt landing. Immense excitement followed. The ambulance rushed about and people waved wheels in the air to tell us what we already knew. We got down without injury and a week later the machine had been repaired and we were flying it again.

Even in this account there is no suggestion of an old soldier's tale. He is so reserved about recounting any event that might be construed as a 'Line Shoot' that he makes no mention of what he did as a Royal Flying Corps pilot on that particular sortie. His three successful bombs and his machine gun may have destroyed a bridge, killed a German General in a staff car, slain a thousand men or exploded harmlessly in a deserted field. We shall never know from his pen. What we can glean from this hairy tale is that he should have been killed three times over on that one flight. When he told the story fifty years after the event he sought no praise or admiration from his readers; he was just making an acknowledgement of his unbelievable good fortune.

Climbing out on the wing indeed, while the Observer tried to maintain straight and level by manipulating two corks attached to the aileron cables where they passed down the fuselage on either side of the rear cockpit. No wonder they got into a spin. The miracle is that it was the bomb and not Lt. Ivelaw-Chapman sans parachute that ended up in the Zillibeke Lake.

Throughout his life he loved to put people into compartments. "The world is divided," he would say, "into those who apologize after colliding with a stranger on a crowded street and those who snarl, 'Get out of my bloody way'." He, along with most of the Edwardian Military Gentlemen, was an apologizer. He would raise his hat and say sorry to a lamp post if he bumped into one after a couple of drinks in the black-out. This is an example of the exaggerated unselfishness which was a characteristic of his generation. They seemed to regard it as a crime to discomfort other people in any way.

There is exaggerated unselfishness in the Zillibeke Lake story. His immediate concern on discovering that he had carried an unexploded bomb back from Hunland and was now faced with the problem of getting rid of it while over Belgium was how to avoid injuring allied civilians on the ground. Other, though not necessarily lesser, men would have made their sole concern at this stage to save themselves and their flying machine; and if the bomb dropped off and killed a Belgian or two or maybe a couple of cows, so be it. This was war. But that was not the way the Chapman/Fletcher team operated.

"My first thought was to dunk ourselves, it, and the aeroplane in the North Sea": this was a suicidal proposal. If the bomb didn't go off on impact and blow them both to smithereens, the machine with its broken undercarriage would have nosed over and certainly the crew would have drowned. But *no one else on the allied side would have been hurt* and that was their primary consideration. In the same way the real triumph of the story from his point of view lies in the words "we gazed down at Zillibeke Lake. More by luck than judgement the bomb fell into it and exploded harmlessly."

Letter home; 3 Sep 1918.

My Dear People,
I have not had a letter since I wrote you last so there is little news. The only reply I got to my letter to Cox's was my pass book. This is sufficient, however, and I have culled the following information. The total sum put to my credit from 29/9/17 to 5/5/18 is £17 3s 8d and the total deduction

23

for income tax is £9 0s 0d. I think this is all the information you require. Yesterday I had a somewhat pleasant surprise; the CO told me that after a bit of judicious wangling he had managed to keep me in the Squadron and that I was to take over B Flight from today. I am therefore now Captain Chapman, complete with three pips, the responsibility of a Flight and a hut to myself where I am now writing this letter. It was only by the sheerest bit of luck that I got it. The late Flight Commander of B Flight went home to England with nerves a week ago. Two days after, a pilot from another squadron was posted in to fill his place but on the very same day he was admitted into hospital and sent to the Base. Then another fellow from another squadron who was senior to me on the promotion list was going to get it. But the CO in conjunction with the Colonel managed to persuade the Brigade to give me the job. Hence my luck in staying with the squadron. Since then I have led a daylight bombing raid into Hunland, bombing bridges; and this morning I was up and shooting up motor transport along the roads when my Observer got hit by machine-gun fire. I sent it down by wireless and everything was waiting on the aerodrome when we landed. We all hoped he had got a 'Soft Blighty'; but I was round the CCS with the CO this afternoon and the MO who admitted him tells me it was a very serious wound indeed, and in a vital spot. The annoying part of it was only three bullets hit the machine at all; two through the planes and the third got poor old Mills. I am very anxious to hear what the Doctor says in the morning when I ring him up. All of what I have been telling you has happened within the last 24 hours. I enclose one (A Photograph) of Yours Humbly in the Bristol Fighter.

Lots of Love,
Ron.

There is significance in "My Dear People". This is the first letter home that opens with this salutation. "My Dear Mother"s there are in abundance along with the classically educated "Dear Mater"s. There are a few, possibly slightly homesick "My Darling Mother"s and now, undoubtedly because of the momentous contents of the letter to follow, we see for the first time "My Dear People". He felt as Captain Chapman DFC of No 10 Squadron, Royal Flying Corps, that he was no longer a junior member of his family whose letters from the Front were on a par with childish scribbles from Scout Camp. Now he was an adult; and his father Joseph, assuming he was home from the Guianas, his sister Eileen and sister Shirley should no longer think of him as a schoolboy.

In the Mess bar that evening, after the most momentous 24 hours in his life, he would have finished his drink and his cigarette and excused himself with a casual remark:

"I'm off to my hut now. I think I'll scribble a line or two to my people in Cheltenham before I turn in. See you all at briefing."

An awestruck newcomer to the Squadron who was unfamiliar with the proper way to address a newly promoted Captain would have probably stood up and replied:

"Good-night, Sir."

Captain Ivelaw-Chapman, DFC was still only 19 years old.

He writes that it was only by the sheerest bit of luck that he was given command of the Flight. But that was not the true message. The good luck lay in the fact that it was Poor Old Mills and not Young Ron that stopped rather more than a 'Soft Blighty' that morning in 1918.

The experience of war seems to have matured without brutalizing him; but we must not imagine that being a pilot in Belgium in 1918 was a carefree existence. He undoubtedly realized that he was riding his luck, but equally he can not have been blind to the horrors that awaited him if it ever ran out. We do not know if his predecessor as Flight Commander was the same "tip-top fellow" who had impressed him so much when he first joined the Squadron, but tip top or not, this man had reached his limit and was "sent home with nerves," and all servicemen know what that means. There is no sign that Ron was near cracking up at any stage, but with his new responsibility he seems to have become a little more serious about life.

The "CCS" was, of course, the Casualty Clearing Station. We can only imagine what such places were like during the final great battles of the First World War, but to have visited one as a healthy young man, to have searched among the blood-stained beds for a close friend and, on finding him, to discover that he was dying must have been a horrific experience. Though he never described it in his writings, that scene was fixed in his memory for the rest of his life. His whole attitude to war and its brutality was coloured by it.

For those of us who have not fought in a war it seems paradoxical that participants in military combat can ever be sorry when it is all over. If war is the ultimate disaster it seems almost immoral to suggest that there are moments when those actually engaged in hostilities are having a wonderful time. If questioned on this subject, most Edwardian Military Gentlemen would suggest that it was not the process of fighting that they enjoyed, but the circumstances in which they found themselves while the war was going on. Freed from the restraint of worrying about the future, Captain Ivelaw-Chapman and his friends could live each day to the full. Under the psychedelic influence of battle, friendships were closer, spirits were higher and parties more boisterous than they ever would be again; and their

Squadron was simply the best fighting unit that the world had ever known. They can be forgiven for acting rather strangely and becoming rather embittered with anti-climax when at the 11th hour of the 11th day of the 11th month in 1918 the First World War was brought to a close.

Letter to his Mother. Signs of the end of the War.

France
November 9th.

My Dear Mater,
    Very many thanks for ripping wire which I'm afraid was only called for by an outburst of melancholie as a result of poor old Mack's death. It arrived just after my last letter had been posted.
    We have had another move and a rattling good one too. We are now lodged in an English Brewer's ex-mansion. In other words a gorgeous jerry-built château complete with Turkish carpets, grand piano, oak panels, billiard table, high ceiling, white table cloths, oak chairs, shallow broad stairs, water laid on in my bedroom, a vast number of mirrors, a small lawn and a conservatory. Long may we stay here. All our Officers are billeted here and we have dinner in the long dining hall. Last night we had a small dance (Men only) in the ball room (Parquet flooring) including a set of Lancers and Sir Roger de Coverley and we ended up with a childish rag-about and charades.
    I do hope we'll be in this château for Armistice Night or Xmas night; oh what a night that would be. My Observer has been slightly wounded while flying with another pilot. I have now got a new fellow who is very keen and efficient. Owing to the Hun retirement I have a lot of interesting news to give you when I get home.
                              Lots of Love,
                              Ron.

What a remarkably well-mannered team of conquering heroes these young men from No 10 Squadron were. There was no ransacking of the chateau cellars; no sorties into town to round up the local girls for an orgy in the ballroom; no looting of silver or vandalizing the picture gallery. They celebrated the final advance of the war and the growing realization that, contrary to all expectations, they were going to survive, by playing charades and dancing the Lancers and Sir Roger de Coverley — with each other.

The Victory Medal to which they were all shortly to become entitled is inscribed 'The Great War for Civilization' and these men were convinced that they had been fighting on the civilized side. The Germans were the

Barbarians. This letter, with its unconscious boyish charm, shows us how deep was the regard for civilized behaviour that was ingrained in the character of the Edwardian Military Gentlemen. If there was any hell-raising to be done, it would involve aeroplanes, where the only property, life or limb that was at risk would be their own.

Letter to his Mother. December 1918, Reychem. (R I-C has received notice of a posting home from France. He has just returned from a visit to Wing Headquarters where he has tried, unsuccessfully to get the posting changed.)

As I returned from Wing this morning I was so fed up with life that I immediately went up in the air (the first time in 3 weeks,) and contrary to all instructions, did all the most foolish stunts I could think of including diving on the CO who was riding on Menin aerodrome and making him get off his horse.

There was tragedy in the making here. Even today the RAF is familiar with, and terrified of, the 'Farewell Beat-Up'; the occasion when a squadron member celebrates his last trip before posting with an undisciplined display over his home airfield. Such beat-ups have been known to go disastrously wrong. A flypast too low; a turn too tight; a slow roll that goes a little awry; any one of these can lead to a funeral instead of a farewell party. Captain Ivelaw-Chapman was, of course, Flight Commander and could therefore authorize himself to fly at any time. We must conclude that on this occasion he was lucky and that his remarkable self-control kept him aware of the dangers of trying just one stunt too many, especially when in such an angry frame of mind.

It was early in December, 1918, that Chaps, OC B Flight of Number 10 Squadron Royal Air Force cut loose a bit from the tight reins of flying discipline and beat the hell out of Menin Airfield. It was not the first occasion. Captain Russell Mallinson, who was squadron adjutant at the time, witnessed a memorable stunt a few weeks earlier almost at the moment of Armistice.

'Our Readers' War-Time Stories.' *Evening News*, December 8th 1931.

"At dawn on November 11th, 1918 on the old German Aerodrome at Staceghem in Flanders, occupied by No 10 Squadron RAF, we spotted our Flight Commander emerging from the recreation hut with a mysterious bulge beneath his leather flying coat. We knew him for a gallant fellow of infinite resource — he was recently decorated — and we scented that he had some final surprise for the Bosch; final because hostilities were to end at 11am. At 11 o'clock we were over the advancing British and French line and it was then that the Flight Commander dropped his surprise from the skies. As a strangely moving silence fell over the battle area, the formation leader's streamered machine dived on our troops and from the cockpit spun...a football.

As it bounced gaily in front of them the Tommies let out their first post-war cheer. In a moment a laughing, boisterous throng of khaki clad figures flung themselves on the ball and two rifles were thrust into the mud to act as goalposts. And so within a minute of the end of the greatest war in history our lads were playing their national game like a pack of youngsters let out of school.

On the left we saw the blue line of the French infantry marching grimly on. Not for them 'Le Sport'.

Sgd. P Russell Mallinson; late Bedfordshire Regt. and RAF."

That was a typical Chaps gesture. Skilful; wonderful timing; unexpected sense of humour; bit of a showman; a man others loved to look up to.

As the Great War came to a close we must consider what made him decide to stay in the Air Force when demobilization was all around him. He had already realized that in wartime the Air Force was little more than an indulgence; a mosquito bite that could only annoy two contestants who were slugging it out with the body blows of conventional warfare. He must have understood that in the high days of peace after the Great War it was unlikely that the RAF could survive solely on an enthusiastic estimate of what it might one day be able to do. And yet he determined to stay in the Service against all sensible advice and with strong opposition from his father who had plans that he should train to be a doctor or perhaps enter the Indian Civil Service.

Some hope. Flying and the military way of life were in this man's blood like a drug. If there was to be an Air Force after 1918, he was going to be in it, and we can not escape the notion that he spent the next 40 years of his life endeavouring to recapture the excitement, the comradeship, the adventure and some of the glory that he enjoyed during the last year of the War To End All Wars.

CHAPTER 4

INDIA

No. 97 Squadron, India. 1919 – 1922.

As soon as I got back to England after my 11 months in France I set myself two aims. First; to get abroad again as soon as I could and second; to get a Permanent Commission in the newly formed Royal Air Force. Father was bitterly disappointed. He had always mapped out for me a degree course at Oxford followed by entry into the Indian Civil Service. However, I was bitten by the 'Flying Bug' and all I wanted was to continue in the art or profession of military aviation. After the excitement and stimulus of 18 months of flying, the majority on active service, I just couldn't tolerate the prospect of returning to academic study and a career in the Indian Civil Service.

While I was still at the Depot at Uxbridge I volunteered for any job that would take me overseas. I remember in particular answering a call for volunteers (Pilots) to go to Russia on some exciting jaunt. But nothing came of that and I was getting a little despondent when there came a call for volunteers for a new squadron that would embark for India in the summer of 1919. This sounded just my 'Cup of Tea' and by August that year I was on board the troopship Mandala *bound for Bombay with a full complement, officers and other ranks of No 97 Squadron due to be equipped with DH 10s on arrival in India.*

There was no noble motive in his volunteering to go to India. He didn't feel himself called to service in the East like so many British men and women during the 400 years of the Indian Empire, nor did he see the troopship to Bombay as an escape from a career in England that had reached a dead end. He went to India for the irresistible prospect of travel, danger and adventure. He was already contemptuous of security as an end in itself and throughout his life he derided those who selected their careers with one eye on a comfortable retirement.

His later writings confirm that he never regretted the decision to pursue the two great aspirations of his life, military aviation and adventure, through the medium of commissioned service in the RAF. If, on occasions, the rather stultifying military way of life was not completely to his liking it never worried him: the game was always worth the candle.

Biographical Notes. Introspection.

Now that I am extolling what I regard to be my better points, I would mention my constant desire to be doing something out of the ordinary; a little unconventional and preferably with a touch of risk to it. In the Book of Common Prayer we say these words; "and grant that this day we fall into no sin, neither run into any kind of danger". Even now at the age of 70 my Amen applies only to the sin; I can not seriously pray for my life to be free from danger.

Biographical Notes. Footnote to 'Some Thoughts on Manned Military Aviation.'

Recently I was offered a stall in the Bath Chapel (Henry VII Chapel in Westminster Abbey) with a view to being installed at a Service to be held in October, 1975. I gladly agreed and in so doing accepted the prospect of becoming armigerous since a stall holder must have his banner and achievements positioned above his stall. The Genealogist of the Order, York Herald of the College of Arms, produced a coat of arms for me 'De Novo' since I had no arms-bearing forebears. Amongst other things York Herald asked me for suggestions as to an appropriate motto. I chose 'Laete Servio'; Gladly do I Serve.

It was in India in 1919 that he started to enjoy his Service.
Biographical Notes. Service Memories. 97 Squadron, India, 1919-1922.

Soon after we got going as a squadron I was chosen as one of the pilots for the first Indian Air Mail service flown between Bombay and Karachi during the winter of 1919/20. We lived in a tented camp sprawled through a palm grove right along the sea at Juhu Island some 10 miles north of Bombay. There were hectic supper and moonlight bathing parties attended by some of the élite of Bombay's European population, including on more than one occasion the two daughters of HE the Governor.

I count myself extremely lucky to have served as part of the British Forces in India during the time that the British Raj was still paramount and unquestioned. Service in India in these conditions was a curious paradox. We lived a pampered life, secure in the feeling of absolute superiority to all natives, no matter what their calling in life. We British led our own rather sheltered lives in Cantonments, with no contact with the Indians about us save those who served us in some menial capacity. There were Bearers, Khitmatgars, Syces, Bhistis, Malis, Dhobis, and many others who worked for us. In return we paid them, I think reasonably well, and we treated them as humans. Many were the long-standing bonds of loyalty and understanding built between Sahib and servant which survived in many cases the Sahib's return to England. But we took few pains to discover what was going on in their minds and merely took their servility and loyalty for granted. 30 years later I was back in India after Independence as C in C of their Air Force. It was only then that I realized to the full how sheltered and in a way unrewarding had been my service in India in the days of the British Raj. During this, my third visit to India in 1949 to 1951 I met for the first time the truly intelligent Indians, most of whom had kept well clear of the British before Independence. I liked the people that I met and formed many lasting friendships among them.

Returning to the years 1919-1922, I saw much of the life so vividly depicted by Kipling; the gymkhanas, the dances, the dinner parties, the guest nights, the picnics, the polo matches, the paper-chases and the Hill Stations with all their local scandal. It was all most enjoyable; it was somehow comforting and the whole package was available at a cost far below its counterpart in England.

He flew an ancient biplane from Lahore to Allahabad. The journey was described in a letter to his family in November, 1919, and again in an article for *Blackwood's Magazine* in 1969. Surprisingly he seemed to think that his parents should be kept in the dark about the illicit night joy-ride over the racecourse at Lucknow, while he left out the stories of the first flight over the Taj Mahal and the amazing 75-year-old Subadar Major from the version presented to the readers of *Blackwoods*.

Blackwoods 1969.

In India in 1919 I was ordered to fly an old tractor biplane, a BE 2C from Lahore to Allahabad. My instructions were to get it there in one piece, no matter how long it took. My first stop was at Ambala for more petrol. Here my passenger walked into the propeller while it was going round and smashed it with his head. He later recovered. I waited a week at Ambala enjoying the halcyon cantonment life of British India until a new propeller arrived, and then pressed on with my mission.

Note that the *first* stop was at Ambala and that he seems to have enjoyed himself during the week he spent there.

Letter to his family. 1919.

The BE 2Cs have been out in this country for about 2 years on service. They were in an appalling condition. In fact we took them from a hangar of 'Scrapped' machines which were shortly to be put on sale to Indian pilots at about £90 or £100 a time. It took us 4 days to get them fit to take to the air at all. Then at 7.30 one morning with one of our mechanics each as passengers, lots of spares, and about 3 days' kit we started on our 780-mile trip to Allahabad. Our first stop was Jellandur [sic]. Maurice Bainbridge found the correct landing ground; I was not so fortunate. I landed in an airfield close to the native city about 7 miles away from Cantonments, and was immediately surrounded by 2000 natives within a few minutes of landing. I had a terrible time with them; they wanted to touch the machine and work the elevator and ailerons up and down, and turn the prop. around....

In the evening a Captain and Mrs Cadell, who were looking after us, took us to the Club. A native band was playing there and Maurice and I had an impromptu dance on the hard tennis court with Mrs Cadell and some other ladies, by the light of some lamps. After that we went back to their bungalow, had a hearty dinner and turned in. The next morning one wheel on Maurice's bus was flat with an irreparable puncture so, much to the amusement of the locals, and with the aid of some Gurkhas who were on guard, we filled the tyre with hay and took off for Ambala.

Chaps was always an inspired bodger-up of unserviceable vehicles. He never had the academic knowledge of a trained engineer but he knew how to combat what he called the natural perversity of mechanical things. He could produce life from an unwilling motor car engine by some device like blowing backwards down a blocked fuel pipe with a foot pump, and once, in a busy Paris boulevard, he revitalized the stalled family Rover by cleaning the plugs with sandpaper stripped from a packet of Swan Vestas.

To a Royal Flying Corps man an irreparable puncture was no problem. Despite the mirth of the onlookers, he had probably filled an aircraft's tyre with hay on many occasions before that slightly hungover morning at Jellandur.

Letter to his Family. 1919. Continued.

Ambala was the only place between Lahore and Allahabad where there was an RAF Squadron. We arrived there and landed on their priceless aerodrome (not a landing ground at all like the other places) and were met by Captain Steele of 114 Squadron. We stayed at his bungalow and messed at the Club. The next morning as we were preparing to depart for Delhi a mechanic who was walking towards my machine with a pair of chocks walked bang into my one and only propeller which was revolving at 600 rpm. His topi took the brunt of the blow — it was smashed to pulp — and his head got the rest. Luckily for the poor lad it did not fracture his skull. It knocked him out for a bit and he reeled on to the floor. I jumped out, picked him up, packed him into a tender and got him down to the hospital. His cut was deep and nasty but not dangerous. We kicked our heels at Ambala with nothing to do for 11 days but send hastening wires to Lahore. On that prop. alone I used 351 words of OHMS express wire. We lived at the club with three days' kit in a small haversack so naturally we were somewhat put out and not over comfortable. It was a miserable time and I consider that those were 11 days of my life wasted.

There is a suspicion of vanity here. We already know that Chaps made a point of never being bored, indeed he often announced, perhaps rather pompously, that in his view boredom was an affliction of the unintelligent. This notion clearly came to him in later life which explains why in the magazine article in 1969 he suggests that he enjoyed the halcyon cantonment life during his 11 days at Ambala while in the 1919 letter he readily admits to his parents that he was bored to tears.

Letter. (Continued).

When the spare propeller eventually arrived we flew on to the aerodrome and new cantonments at Delhi, 11 miles out of Delhi proper. During the morning I saw a native officer Subadar Major at the Orderly Room who was 75 years old and who had been in the army for 55 years; a fine example of a native soldier. It suddenly struck me that I wanted to take him up. So he was asked and agreed and was told to be at the aerodrome at 5pm. In the evening after a good tiffin and sleeping in the afternoon we went down to the aerodrome. Maurice took up two British Officers. I took up the O.C. first of all and flew him over Delhi to take some photographs from the air. Then I got this Subadar Major, Sera Singh by name, into the machine — he was fifteen stone — strapped him in and took off. I was sitting behind and thoroughly enjoyed the pantomime. First of all he sat very tight, holding on with both hands. Then he found he didn't fall out so he sat up and took a little notice. Then I flew him over the men's parade ground and at this he was quite bucked. I landed him safely and then his OC asked him if he enjoyed it. "Oh yes," he said. Then he was asked if he was frightened. "Oh no," he said, "Before I go up I leave everything on the ground." He had divested himself of his Sam Browne and Pugree and all his earthly

*possessions and heirlooms and handed them to a Sepoy before going up. "I
put myself in Sahib's hand," he said. "If Sahib breaks, I break too."
Quite a sound philosophy. He was far and away the oldest person I have
ever taken up. The next morning we were up by 6, took off about 7am,
dived down on the Punjabi's parade ground, waved goodbye and then off
to Agra, about 110 miles. We did this in about an hour and ten minutes.
When we got there I came down while my mechanic took a photograph of
the Taj Mahal from the air. It was a wonderful sight with the sun on it.
We landed here and were met by an Officer of the 69th Punjabis. He put
us up in the Mess. After our tiffin I went down to the Taj and went all
over it. It is beyond description and I felt absolutely selfish when I saw
it.*

*I wanted everybody I knew or cared for to come and enjoy looking at it
with me. In the evening I took up our host, a Captain Minchin, for a
joy-ride and showed him the Taj from the air just before dusk. He said he
had seen the Taj on several occasions; by day with the sun, by day
without and by moonlight when it is supposed to be the most impressive
sight imaginable, but he had never seen it looking so beautiful as it did
just on dusk from the air where one saw it as its unadorned self without
any borrowed brilliancy, with nothing but the mist rising from the Jumna
to show it off. Both he and I were absolutely wonderstruck.*

The letter then tells of a short hop to Cawnpore where he attended
another *Thé Dansant* with a native band playing at the Officers' Club and
concludes rather abruptly as follows:

*The next morning we pushed off at 7am and covered the last 120 miles to
Allahabad in an hour and a half without any further matter of interest.
Well I've got you to Allahabad and it is now 12.30 am and I have yet to
go to the station and get this posted; so will say good night.*
   Lots of Love
     Yours Wearily,
      Ron.

It is certainly only a short hop from Cawnpore to Allahabad but not if you
go via Lucknow. It appears that he made an unnecessary detour after
Cawnpore to take in Race Week at the famous garrison town of Lucknow.
He was already on what servicemen know as a wonderful 'Swan'. He was
making his way totally unsupervised across half of India and no superior
officer could really know where he was or when he could be expected
back. He was fêted everywhere he landed because of the novelty of the
machine he was flying and his generosity with joy-rides to all and sundry.

Perhaps he still remembered the First World War mail censors and chose not to mention the Lucknow outing in the letter to his parents in case retribution finally caught up with him, but fifty years later it didn't matter who found out.

Blackwoods Magazine. An Incident in Lucknow.

> *"Once more in the air I worked my way on down, hop by hop to Lucknow where my visit coincided with the four days of festivities known as Race Week. There I'm afraid I rather disgraced myself. My first fall from grace was to take up the Governor's daughter — disguised in a suit of overalls — for a flight round the countryside. Unauthorized passengers, particularly those of the fair sex were frowned upon and often became a court martial offence; but who cares at the age of 20? After joy-riding a series of local dignitaries for a couple of days I firmly said I must be on my way. But there was to be a stupendous firework display on the Saturday night to mark the end of Race Week. Couldn't I stay and let them see an aeroplane flying by night? That was too much for me for although I had not done much night flying myself I had been told there was nothing to it and in any case there was a full moon at the time. I was worried that no one would see the aeroplane with all the fireworks whizzing off round it, so with the help of an electrically minded Sapper I rigged a 12-volt battery in the front seat and a string of fairy lights all round the edge of the bottom plane. It was most irregular and a bit rash but it worked all right and I suppose my real aim was achieved much later that evening when I got quite an ovation in the bar of the gymkhana club. Conscience then prevailed and the next afternoon I delivered my B.E. 2C safely at Allahabad aerodrome."*

It is immediately noticeable when reading his stories from India in the early 1920s that there is no mention of what his squadron actually did during the three years that he was out there. There is as much significance in what is omitted as in what he chose to record. The fourth in his impressive array of medals at that time was the India General Service Medal. It has bars for 3 separate campaigns that he was involved in between 1919 and 1923, all fought on the North-West Frontier. The British Government does not issue campaign medals unless bullets are fired in anger and there have to be a minimum number of actual casualties before a campaign is designated medal worthy. So, while his vivid memories are of the sights, sounds and off-duty pleasures of India, where are the stories of blood and thunder on the Khyber Pass? How were the frail aircraft of No 97 squadron actually used against the wild and pitiless men of the Afghan Hills who constantly harassed the garrisons of British India? We shall never know from his journal. The actions for which the medal and its 3 bars were awarded do not rate a mention in a single letter or in one line of memoirs and there is not a photograph in his extensive collection of himself or his squadron on a war footing in India.

There are two conclusions to be drawn from this. First, he was not and was never to be a 'Wog Basher', a distasteful phrase used to describe a type of British serviceman who took pleasure in campaigning against poorly equipped native soldiers. Secondly we can consider this as a reminder that for most adventurous young men of the day military service was an excuse, a vehicle for travel at the country's expense and an opportunity to sample life in another man's world. If, occasionally, they had to knuckle down to a bit of fighting it was a necessary evil, but soon done with and nothing, literally, to write home about. What he did write home about was the Taj Mahal by moonlight and *Thés Dansant* at the Club and a wonderful 6-week trek through the foothills of the Himalayas.

Biographical Notes. India 1919 − 1922

It was while I was stationed at Risalpur that I became very friendly with Tony Shortt, a Lieutenant in the Bengal Sappers and Miners who chanced to be living in the same Mess. A 'David and Jonathan' relationship sprang up between Tony and me that was to last a lifetime. Tony was musical, artistic, well read, athletic, a good horseman; in fact all the things that I was not. Nevertheless I seemed to complement him in some things and we soon discovered that we had much in common in our general outlook on life. At any rate we became inseparable companions and spent every moment of our leisure in each other's company, either arguing, philosophizing or improving the other's mind (as we thought). When it came to planning a bit of local leave during the coming hot weather we decided to go together on a rather lengthy trek which would take us from Srinagar in Kashmir to Dalhousie in the Punjab. It was quite an ambitious schedule as it entailed some 250 miles on our flat feet passing through some of the lower slopes of the Karakoram mountains. During the six weeks that we were trekking we were never on the flat for more than half a mile at a time and we varied in height from sea level to 7000 feet.

We originally intended to combine this trip with a "Shikar", or shooting expedition, as there was plenty of game to be taken along the route. We soon discovered that this was a mistake. To start with I was a terrible shot and Tony wasn't much better. But apart from that it soon became clear that we had set ourselves too ambitious a timetable to combine a mountain trek with a shikar. Our Shikari was forever urging us to stay in this or that camp "for another 3 days" because he was sure that would give us time to stalk some ibex that he heard were in the district. We on the other hand looked at our map, the distance we had yet to cover and the date our leave expired. Though as a shooting party it was a failure, from all other aspects our trek was a great success. We passed through mountain scenery of ever changing beauty and visited many places little frequented by Europeans. Above all we got ourselves immensely fit and at the end could average 5 miles per hour up or down hill over steep gradients. There is another aspect of this trip that must be recorded. One evening in our tent, Tony started describing to me his family at home in England and mentioned his sister who was then aged eleven. I was seized with the romantic idea that if a David and Jonathan friendship sincerely existed between two men there was at least a chance that Jonathan and David's sister might hit it off as man and wife. I pigeonholed that little thought at the back of my mind because there was nothing that could be done about it with me in India and the Shortt family thousands of miles away at Shortlands in Kent. However, a year or eighteen months later back in the UK I made it my first pleasure to call upon the Shortt family and meet the little sister, by then at the advanced age of twelve. A few days later she dined with me at my Club and I came to the conclusion that those romantic ideas conceived in the glorious mountain scenery of the Karakoram might not be quite so dotty after all. Naturally we had to wait a bit but we were eventually married 8 years later on 12th June 1930. Since then never a day passes without my blessing that crazy romantic thought that entered my head one evening during the mountain trek with Tony Shortt in 1921.

He wrote very little about relationships. He was scornful of 'Amateur Psychiatrists' who read deep meanings into all close alliances. Writing, as he was, in the late sixties when permissiveness was what everyone talked about; when a sexual connotation was automatically applied to the most innocent of pairings, he still didn't feel the need to explain that this David and Jonathan relationship was quite platonic. Of course it was. Could anyone imagine anything different? He recorded his deep affection for Tony Shortt with the same endearing innocence that he described the young pilots of the Royal Flying Corps dancing with each other on the eve of the Armistice.

We have learnt that he was no athlete but he was always proud of his stamina. He liked to be fit and to have great reserves of endurance. When he says that while trekking in India he could average 5 miles per hour over any terrain we can be certain that this figure was precisely calculated. He would have measured his marching pace to the nearest inch, counted the paces to the hour, averaged the hours walked in a day and deduced a marching speed. The distance covered would be measured against the miles still to be crossed and the whole equation applied against the amount of leave time available. Tony, the Engineer, would probably have produced a slide rule and at the end of a day's march the two men would decide on whether they had time to sit and watch the wonder of a Himalayan sunset or if they should cover a few more miles before dark. Small wonder that they never had time to shoot anything.

Chaps did have an extraordinary ability to pace himself and to endure. In later years when we read of him resisting torture or showing great strength while suffering from injuries or serious disease we will find that he is always timing himself; measuring his performance and rationing his stamina. During his final illness he kept a log of his failing strength by studiously recording the number of shuffling steps that it took him to walk from the garden gate to the front door.

He was an introspective man even in those early days in India. He analysed his feelings as often as he tested his skills and his strength. There were few experiences during the 3-year tour in India that depressed him. He showed no signs of what is now known as culture shock and he records no unease at the poverty, dirt and malnutrition that must have confronted him every day that he was in India. Edwardian gentlemen were much less troubled with social conscience than we are. Their indifference to the privations of millions of underprivileged Indians was not callous but pragmatic. Suffering with the natives achieved nothing. They after all were them, and we, thank God, were us.

Tony Shortt went on to serve with gallantry and distinction in the Second World War. In the postwar years he held important diplomatic posts in Greece and Australia and was Director of Military Intelligence. He retired as a General and he and Chaps were close friends until the late 1970s when they died within a year or two of each other.

The next story, concerning death by Crossley Tender, was written in 1971. In the script he used the present tense as though the events of fifty years ago were a recurring nightmare.

Biographical Notes. Introspection.

...Now we are in the confessional box it seems the right time and place to confess that I killed a woman once. I am not proud of the circumstances. The year is 1919. I am serving as a subaltern in a flight detachment of No 97 Squadron in India. Our Flight is in camp under coconut palms on Juhu island some 16 miles north of Bombay. We collect our rations daily in a Crossley Tender from a railhead 10 miles towards Bombay. We officers, I think there were five of us, are not supposed to drive the Crossley, but we do; partly because we like to and partly because we think we are better at the job than the two MT drivers posted on our detachment. On this occasion I am driving, probably much too fast, through the bazaar of an Indian

village when I hit a native woman and she died at once. At the civil court case that followed some of the Indian witnesses proclaimed that the noise of the Crossley was like a 'Hawa Jehaz' — an aeroplane — whilst another, a relative, testified that his grandmother was stone deaf. Presumably on that score I escaped the punishment that was my due. But the memory of the event has lived with me ever since and has, I hope, affected the way that I have driven motor cars in the intervening 50 years.

It did affect the way he drove a motor car. He never ceased to remind himself and anyone else he thought would benefit from his experience that a motor car in motion was a lethal weapon. As such the driver was acting with dangerous irresponsibility if anything was allowed to reduce the total concentration that was needed for the job in hand. When, in the 1950s he finally conceded that a radio could be fitted in the family Rover he would not have it switched on while he was driving. "Some people can concentrate on two things at once," he would say, "but I am not one of them." When touring in Brittany or Scotland the car was on occasions brought to a halt and solemnly parked in open country or a lay-by to grant Lady Ivelaw-Chapman the indulgence of 'Mrs Dale's Diary'. What would he have thought of a car phone?

India had a profound influence on the characters of the Edwardian Military Gentlemen. They lived with the notion that the British were destined to rule India for as far into the future as anyone could see and that an army of British fighting men would always be stationed there. Over a period of two hundred years the Indian Army evolved its own way of life and its particular moral code. Young men like him, in India for the first time, took the Indian Army way of doing things as their own. There was no room for liberality in their relations with the natives. Indians had their place and it wasn't within the British cantonments. Men who fraternized too closely with the local inhabitants were accused of having 'Gone Native' and were sent home on the next boat. A military man dealt with the heat in the time-honoured way; lots to drink but easy on the spirits; topi to be worn at all times and spend as much of the hot weather as possible on leave in the mountains. A British soldier should always be in control of himself; it was an iron self-discipline that kept the army sane in India. Don't get worked up; don't complain about the heat; don't buck the system; don't make waves. Remember you're British. Set the natives an example; noblesse oblige; the white man's burden.

Perhaps the strangest cantonment convention was the Indian Army's attitude towards European women. When he left India, Lt Ivelaw-Chapman, who at 27 was a handsome, attractive and healthy man had probably never kissed a girl and certainly never made love to one. He wasn't worried by this state of affairs nor did he suffer the tortures of suppressed lust which are supposed, these days, to afflict young men for whom celibacy extends past their teens. Cantonment rules stated that European women were off limits until marriage had at least been proposed and sari-clad native girls were about as far out of bounds for young officers as the Army could put them. 'So, what did they do?' one wonders. That iron self-discipline was probably the answer. Don't make waves; stick to the rules; remember you're British, and some day maybe you'll marry the first girl you dance with at a Mess Ball, whose mother finds you slightly less than totally unsuitable. Or, if you are Ivelaw-Chapman, you fall in love with a dream. A dog-eared photo of the eleven year old sister of your best army friend, viewed by the light of a paraffin lamp in a tent when 15 days' march into the Karakoram foothills, is enough. You have seen your future wife. You need look no further.

The final subject that we should study in the Indian apprenticeship of the Edwardian Military Man is the way he copes with Death. Death was never very far away from the cantonments of Peshawar and Risalpur – death in battle, death from disease and death that was due to the reality that nature had not prepared Britons to survive in India. The Army was acquainted with Death. There were time-honoured rituals to cope with it; the muffled drum; the Last Post; Rest on your arms reversed; 'They're Hanging Danny Deever in the Morning'. Tradition was designed to replace emotion when a comrade was lost in any cause that might be considered patriotic. And the enemy dead, be they Huns, Pathans, Waziris or whatever, were but statistics the moment they were buried. Kipling again;

> 'When first under fire and you're wishful to duck
> Don't look nor take heed at the man that is struck.
> Be thankful you're living and trust to your luck,
> And march to your front like a soldier.'

True to form Chaps makes no mention in his reminiscences of comrades killed in action or lost from disease. We know that he killed men in the First World War and many of his close friends became casualties. There is little doubt that in India he was operating close behind the guns in the Third Afghan War. He must have seen corpses and wounded on both sides but they are all expunged from his memory with traditional military finality. Not so the native woman accidentally run down during a boyish joy-ride in a Crossley tender who became a nightmare that haunted him for another fifty years.

And in 1922, after three years in India, as a young man who had added travel to combat in his inventory of life's great experiences, young Chaps sailed from Bombay, bound once more for England.

CHAPTER 5

HOME POSTINGS

From 1923 to 1929 Flying Officer R. Ivelaw-Chapman, D.F.C, R.A.F. served on various units in England. He was a test pilot with the Aircraft and Armament Experimental Establishment at Martlesham Heath near Ipswich and an ordinary squadron pilot on two multi-engined night bomber squadrons. During this period there were no letters to his mother and very few to his teenage girlfriend. His reports and anecdotes were short and strictly factual. He asserted constantly that he enjoyed the flying. It was as though he was trying to convince himself many years later that he had a good time in the early twenties and led a worthwhile existence. But the Royal Air Force in those days can not have been much fun. The outbreak of Peace in Europe and the great Depression at home meant that Defence Expenditure was low. Flying hours were limited and officer's pay was actually reduced; but worst of all there seems to have been a lack of direction. No one seemed certain what sort of Air Force was needed, and what its aims and tasks were to be. There seems to have been no career structure during this period. Literally hundreds of young men with war records as brilliant as Chaps's milled around the lower ranks of the RAF apparently unconcerned about their future employment as long as they could occasionally get the injection of open cockpit air time on which they were all dependant. We should remember that it was these young men who were to be the Squadron, Wing and Station commanders in the early years of the Second World War; the backbone of experience and discipline that controlled the brilliance of the young pilots of 1940. The Notes give us a rather unexpected view of what a regular RAF Officer was doing around 1924.

His first flying job in England involved the rudimentary flight testing of some of the hundreds of strange machines that the Air Ministry chose to commission.

Biographical Notes. Martlesham Heath.

I suppose I spent four and a half of the happiest years of my bachelor life at Martlesham Heath, the Aeroplane and Armament Experimental Establishment. I was a test pilot on B Flight (The Heavies). I enjoyed flying the large variety of types that came our way but I was never a success

*in the real technique of test flying. I did all my serious work in my own
flight (the multi-engined giants of the day) but there were also aeroplanes
in the single-seater flight that we were invited to fly as the opportunity
offered. I flew a vast range of aircraft, many of which never passed the
prototype stage. During my 3 years at Martlesham I flew no less than 78
different types including the Dormouse, Hamilton, Cygnet, Yeovil,
Berkeley, Springbok, Vespa, Bugle, Hendon, Cubaroo, Possum, Wolf,
Handcross, Bodmin, Ava, Awana, Weasel, and Derby.*

*We used to take off with a knee pad strapped outside our flying kit to
which a stop watch was fitted and I always carried a spare stop watch on
a string round my neck because I often dropped the first one. The test flights
often took us up as high as 21,000 feet. Oxygen was not available and the
cold was intense. Cockpits were unheated and always open to the wind.*

It was one of his vanities in later years to display the distorted arthritic first
joint of his right hand index finger as though it was a war wound. "That's
from frostbite," he'd say. "I got that flying at 20,000 feet in an open cockpit.
I took my glove off to write on my knee pad and this finger froze onto the
gold pencil I was using. I thawed it out in front of the fire in the Mess Bar
about an hour later. I get something extra on my pension for being arthritic,
you know." He probably wasn't a great success as a test pilot, but he
certainly had style, making notes with a gold pencil at 20,000 feet without
oxygen in the open cockpit of an aeroplane with a strange name like
"Cubaroo".

Carefully pasted into one of the scrapbooks is the programme for the Royal
Air Force Aerial Pageant at Hendon in 1924. It is a marvellously nostalgic
document. The cover is early Art Deco with a coloured picture of a twin
engined biplane climbing away from a successful bombing attack on a
smoking bridge. The advertisements are for 9-cylinder rotary engines and
war-surplus Bristol Fighters. There is a photo of a Parnall Possum, an
aerodynamic non-starter that figured in Chaps' Martlesham log book. The
machine has three open cockpits, three wings, three wheels, two propellers
and one engine. The 450 HP Napier Lion is mounted in the fuselage and the
drive to the propellers is by bevel gear. If it ever took off it is hard to imagine
that it climbed high enough to give a test pilot frostbite. His log book reveals
that Chaps' total flying time in the Possum was less than 10 minutes. Even
that would seem to have been something of an achievement.

The Hendon Pageant was really a military version of the Flying Circus and
was obviously designed to let the public know how the defence budget was
being spent. However, the aeroplane as a fighting machine is notoriously
difficult to display. The aircraft on show can not actually drop bombs or fire
bullets. Pilots have to fight mock battles which come over as rather puerile,

and they are made to take part in competitions which are ludicrously contrived.

From the Hendon Programme; 1924.

"It is assumed that there are high trees over the area occupied by the spectators and therefore anyone flying over this area will be disqualified. The winner will be the pilot who, in the opinion of the judges executes the best and safest landing within the enclosure. Pilots must switch off at 1000 feet and any pilot who uses his engine after switching off, touches the hedge with any part of his machine or damages any part of his machine in landing will be disqualified."

Nineteen pilots, one from every RAF Flying Station, entered for this competition. Twelve of these held medals for gallantry in the First World War, and Biggin Hill was represented by Squadron Leader Sir C.J.Q. Brand, KBE, DSO, MC, DFC., who must surely have been an officer of some distinction before reverting to lowly rank in the RAF and devoting his military skills to the Great Hendon Forced Landing Competition.

Item 13 (From the Programme) 5.40 pm.

"Destruction of a Bridge. An important railway bridge in unsettled territory is protected by a small military post. The post is heavily attacked by hostile troops. A wireless telegraph message is received at our RAF Headquarters to the effect that the post can not possibly hope to hold out longer than a few hours. It is determined to evacuate the post and destroy the bridge. Three Vickers Vernons escorted by 5 single-seat fighters are dispatched and the former land near the bridge..."

The third Vickers Vernon was flown by Flying Officer R Ivelaw- Chapman D.F.C.

Biographical Notes. Anecdotes section. The Vickers Vernon at Hendon Air Pageant.

In the early 1920s one of the big events of the year was the annual air pageant at Hendon. In 1924 I was taking part in a Set Piece which ended the show. I was flying a Vickers Vernon troopcarrier. I had a full load of 14 soldiers in the cabin and my task was to land at Hendon. As soon as the machine came to a halt — no wheel brakes — out rushed the troops and blew up a dummy Fort erected on the aerodrome. Then they hurried back on board, slammed the door and off we went. The Producer had asked me to give the event maximum realism by taking off from where I had come to a halt instead of taxying back to the edge of the aerodrome to get the best possible take-off run. Thus my available take-off distance was halved and I needed all the power that I could get from my two engines to clear the treetops with my heavy load. I opened the throttles as soon as all the troops were back on board and the doors closed, and we got into the air comfortably before I reached the public enclosure. There was a tremendous crowd that year and I could see them immediately below me. But, when I was at about 50 feet and climbing, both engines cut dead and I began to sink. There was nothing for it but to keep straight on whilst trying to locate the trouble. A glance around the cockpit showed that the main magneto switches for both engines were in the Off position. I clicked them on and, by the Grace of God, both engines responded and I climbed away once more from within feet of the heads of the crowd. How could such a thing have happened? Easily. I was wearing leather gauntlets. On the back of each glove was an extra flap which could be brought forward to cover the fingers like a mitten in very cold weather. On this occasion the flaps were buttoned back. When I opened the throttles with my right hand the flap on my gauntlet had caught the master magneto switches and knocked them off. Within a week of this incident the magneto switches on all Vernons had been repositioned outside the cockpit and out of harm's way.

Chaps occasionally added a rider to this tale. Apparently in the centre of the public enclosure was the Royal Box and seated therein was the second son of King George V who was patron of the Hendon Pageant. The fully loaded and suddenly very silent Vickers Vernon dived at the Duke of York with the lethality of an assassin's bullet and only when a disaster seemed inevitable did the engines cough and pick up again. The Duke, unsure as to whether this manoeuvre was intentional, apparently applauded weakly. The Chapman good luck was once again to the fore and the future King of England had a remarkable escape.

The mistakes that a man survives are known as experience.

The 'Producer' referred to in the text who was so keen to sacrifice safety for dramatic effect was the head of the Flying Committee, named in the programme as Air Commodore Dowding, who, fifteen years later, led Fighter Command in the Battle of Britain.

Biographical Notes. Martlesham Heath.

While at Martlesham I spent some time as Adjutant of the Station and worked in close contact with the C.O., Wing Commander Napier John Gill who was one of the most interesting characters I have ever met. He had a clear and incisive brain and had written a book on aerodynamics while still a subaltern in the Gunners. He had a complete inability to suffer fools and a biting tongue on occasions, but at heart he was as human as one could wish for. He was blessed with a lovely sense of humour and his wit was always couched in unforgettable language. I remember this story about him. There was an Officers' Mess Ball. Napier Gill was unaccompanied and did not dance but he stayed till the end of the evening sipping his favourite Irish whiskey and chatting to some of the guests at the bar. Finally when he felt he had done his duty as C.O. he decided to leave. At the cloakroom he asked a rather obsequious Sergeant steward for his hat and gloves. "Certainly Sir, and what is the name?" the man replied. "My name is Gill; Napier John; Wing Commander; Church of England and men who don't recognize me get shot at dawn. Now give me my hat, you bloody fool." My respect for Gill amounted almost to hero worship. Unfortunately his fondness for Irish and water cut short what would otherwise have been a brilliant career in our service.

There are some deductions to be made from this anecdote which at first sight seems rather pointless and unfunny. Fifteen years later, after the outbreak of the Second World War, Chaps proved to be an outstanding military leader. Because he joined the Service during the First War and had no formal officer training at a military academy we must assume that he learned leadership by observation and imitation. When he was in command he deliberately cultivated aspects of the demeanour of commanders that had impressed him; the worldliness of Major Keith Murray of the R.F.C.; the charisma of Napier Gill and even some of the philosophy of his schoolmasters. The charisma of command is a combination of carefully calculated mannerisms and an innate power of personality. The whole ritual of a military chain of command is designed to stress the duty of some men to give orders and others to obey them without question.

In the story the Sergeant fails to recognize his commander. That is a situation that should not occur and is in some ways an indictment of Wing Commander Gill. The *raison d'être* of military parades is to familiarize the rank and file with their commanders so that they know whose voice to obey in the heat of battle. The Wing Commander's immediate response is to display like a peacock; to create enough of a scene to ensure that the Sergeant will never again have to ask his Commander's name. He then gives an order; "Give me my hat, you bloody fool." Military commanders are not permitted to say "Please". There must be no confusion between an order and a request. Even after a Mess Ball when slightly the worse for the Irish Whiskey a

Commander's orders must be blunt, unquestionable and overbearing to the point of arrogance. The successful commander, however, the man who truly has the charisma of command, can deliver his orders with all the required firmness and yet nullify any suggestion of ill will by subtle eye-contact and conciliatory gesture. The military gentlemen of this era knew from a very early age how to give orders, how to lead and to inspire confidence and Chaps seems to have picked up most of the art from his CO at Martlesham Heath.

Thus we see him through most of the 1920s. He was a good pilot, but by no means brilliant, and the next two stories about his adventures while flying the Handley Page Hyderabad show a tendency towards indiscipline which would have led to court martial in later days. He was still pursuing single mindedly his affair with Betty Shortt as she progressed through the classes at Bromley High School for Girls and at work he was laying the foundations of experience on which his career was built. There were undoubtedly times when he suffered from the ennui which is part and parcel of a military man's life during home postings in peacetime but on the whole he was happy and not remotely ambitious for promotion in the Service.

Biographical Notes. Anecdotes. A Near Thing at North Coates.

In the summer of 1926 after I had spent 5 years at Martlesham Heath I was with No 99 Squadron at Bircham Newton in Norfolk. We were flying a relatively big twin-engined aircraft called the Hyderabad made by Handley Pages at Cricklewood. No. 99 was a Night Bomber Squadron and we carried air gunners who had to practise firing air to ground. Part of the summer training was to fly up to North Coates in Lincolnshire where there was a range with targets set up on the foreshore. I had every pilot's love for low flying and this stretch of sand was a constant temptation to which I often succumbed. One morning I was haring along the beach at nought feet and about 150 miles per hour without proper heed to what I was doing. The result was that I hit the ground a glancing blow with my undercarriage and bent it rather badly. Having bounced back into the air I was forced to do some quick thinking. A crash landing of some sort was now inevitable and it was beyond the resources of the squadron to repair a damaged aircraft of this size. I had achieved what the manuals call a 'Maker's Rebuild'. I realized that I would be very unpopular with the Squadron if I dumped on them a Hyderabad which they would have to dismantle and transport on a fleet of lorries to the maker's factory. So I wrote a message [with a gold pencil no doubt] confessing my guilt and explaining things to my Commanding Officer, and dropped it at Squadron HQ. In the message I asked permission to fly on to Handley Page's aerodrome at Cricklewood in North London and deliver the damaged

Hyderabad directly to the works manager there who would have to undertake the repair anyway. Unfortunately it was Saturday and early closing at the factory and despite an urgent plea from my CO they flatly refused to take delivery. So I had to crash land ignominiously at my home station of Bircham Newton. Surprisingly the CO did not exact the penalties I richly deserved. He seemed to have been appeased by my initiative in trying to save the squadron engineers some trouble.

The RAF still uses the range at North Coates for gunnery, bombing and rockets. In the 1960s pilots regularly succumbed to the temptation to test their skill and their nerve by flying along the sands as low as they dared and then a little lower. Between Chaps's day and the present there have probably been a few that overdid things and actually bounced their machines off terra firma. There will not have been many, however, who survived the incident and the subsequent crash landing unscathed, came through the disciplinary proceedings without catastrophic loss of seniority and went on to become Vice Chief of the Air Staff. In 1926 his luck had not deserted him, nor had romance.

Biographical Notes. Martlesham Heath 1922-1926.

For the whole of my time at Martlesham and at Bircham, I was engaged in what I can only term "Unilateral Wooing". Margaret [Betty of the last chapter] lived with her people in Beckenham in Kent and was completely ignorant − or so I succeeded in kidding myself − of my set purpose in life. For me, watching her grow from 12 to 16 merely confirmed that I had made no mistake in my choice of my future wife, however long I had to wait for her. Martlesham lies on the north east side of Ipswich in Suffolk; Beckenham is well south of the Thames. I found the answer in Terence the Trusty Triumph − my 3½ H.P. motorbike − which would cover the intervening distance in about three hours including a crossing on the Woolwich Ferry and wending my way through miles of dockland before reaching the Romford to Ipswich main road. Many was the time that I left Margaret's home on Terence about midnight on a Sunday for the journey back to Martlesham with the thought of an 8am parade on Monday morning.

In 1928 he was still a junior pilot on a night bomber squadron. Ten years after the end of the Great War he had regained neither the command of a Flight nor his Royal Flying Corps' acting rank of Captain. He seems to have passed his days driving round the country on a motorbike, and the nights carrying out rather aimless cross-country flights in his Hyderabad. The next anecdote tells of a hairy moment over Lincolnshire. It illustrates the point that the aircrew of the day made their greatest contribution to the development of military aviation by getting involved in and surviving the cock-ups that beset any new science. These were the men who found out the hard way that pilots simply can not fly without reference to a real or artificial horizon; that without electronic aids nine out of ten navigators will fail to find a target on a moonless night; that air to ground communication must be more reliable than notes scribbled with gold pencils and dropped over the edge of an open cockpit. Then, the necessity having been proved, invention would follow. Flight instruments and radio compasses, Radar, Navaids and even the air to ground radio were developed as a result of the trouble men like Flying Officer Ivelaw-Chapman and his navigator got into without them.

Biographical Notes. Anecdotes. 'A Hairy Night Over the Midlands.'

I flew a Hyderabad by daylight from Upper Heyford to Catterick. I was authorized to take off at 10pm for the return flight. The Commanding Officer of our Squadron, Wing Commander Smythies, elected to come with me on this flight as second pilot cum navigator. For the first part of the return flight all went well but our course took us directly over the Midlands factory area and almost without warning I found myself flying in thick Midlands smog. This was in the days before instrument flying and once one had lost sight of the horizon one had no means other than feel of judging one's attitude in the air. Soon after I ran into this smog, things started happening. I tried to climb through it but my airspeed indicator told me that instead I was gathering speed, which meant that I was not being very clever; levelling off, I tried a turn in an effort to get out of it sideways, but all that happened was that my compass started spinning and that meant that I was close to losing control of the aircraft altogether. We had originally been flying on a southerly course and I realized that the only thing to do was to get back to a northerly heading, get clear of the smog and do a proper re-think. I managed to get a grip on things then and by easing the Hyderabad round five degrees at a time and settling on each course I eventually got her back on north and a quarter of an hour later I was clear of the smog at about 11,000 feet somewhere over the Midlands, but neither of us were at all sure where. Looking at my fuel gauge it was now clear that we couldn't get back to Catterick or on to Upper Heyford.

Although we had emerged into clear air I could not see the ground as it was completely obscured by ground mist. So I decided to turn east because I felt certain that despite the mist I would be able to pick up the east coast when we reached it and I knew that well enough to edge my way along to my old station at Bircham Newton where I felt that they would take me down. After 20 minutes of an easterly course there suddenly loomed up below us the glow in the cloud of the lights of quite a sizeable town. I circled the lights for a time and my CO passed me a note asking me what I made of it. I replied that it was probably either Lincoln or Louth. [Lincoln, with the cathedral on top of the hill, has already figured in Chaps's navigational experience. Even on the murkiest night the obstruction lights on the twin towers should have been unmistakable.] *My navigator agreed and soon handed me a note: "Steer 120 degrees for Cranwell." I swung over to this new course and we soon cleared the belt of ground mist and I could pick out ground features quite well. Within 10 minutes I saw what, by the regularity of the street lighting, I guessed to be an army or RAF camp; more probably RAF because of the red obstruction light on one of the buildings. I circled the camp for quite a while, gradually losing height, in the firm belief that we had reached Cranwell. Soon I saw some activity from M.T. vehicles and at long last, the light of a single paraffin flare in the darkness of what I assumed was the landing ground. Soon there was another flare and then a complete flarepath. I made one more circuit and landed. We weren't at Cranwell but at Digby; a few miles away.*

We owed our rescue to the Station Duty Officer at Digby. My old friend Reggie Lydford, on tottering out of the bar at closing time, had heard the sound of a large twin-engined aircraft circling overhead and organized the flarepath which had quite literally saved our lives. He and I had a drink together before turning in. I confessed to him that I had about 3 minutes' fuel left when the wheels finally touched down at Digby. My Squadron Commander was, by this time, quite speechless.

Reggie Lydford became Sir Harold and succeeded Chaps as Commander-in-Chief, Home Command in 1952.

Pilots will know that since the 1930s a whole organization has been made available to ensure that aircraft flying at night never get into the situation that confronted this crew. The full met. briefing before take off; the destination airfield landing forecast; the planned diversion airfield with all landing aids switched on; the airfield identification beacon, direction finding...the radio; all are nowadays considered vital before even the shortest transit flight after dark. Yet Chaps and his CO were totally unprepared and unbriefed when they launched themselves into the darkness from Catterick and so nearly lost their lives. Were they overconfident or careless? Were they disobeying operating procedures or had operating procedures just not been invented? Who knows? What is certain is that the RAF had only ten years left in which to sort out the haphazard nature of night flight and produce aircraft and crews who could survive in the dark, let alone locate a target and attack it.

Biographical Notes.

In 1928 I was still pursuing the unilateral wooing that I mentioned earlier. By this time I was 29 and Margaret (Betty) was coming up for eighteen. I was still determined to marry her but I wanted to wait and see whether she, once old enough to form a proper opinion on the subject, would be willing to marry me. I also wanted to put both of us to the test of separation from each other. So, soon after getting to Upper Heyford, I volunteered for overseas service during the coming trooping season. I had no idea what the answer would be, Egypt, Palestine, Iraq, Singapore, Hong Kong or back to India. It mattered not to me since my object was to achieve 2 years' enforced separation between Margaret and myself. In fact I could not have been luckier; the posting was to No 70 Squadron in Iraq.

It is interesting to speculate what a modern Agony Aunt would have suggested if Betty Shortt had asked for advice in 1929. She would probably have been told that her man was running away from a serious relationship and that she should forget him if she could not negotiate a formal engagement before his departure.

The person who really needed advice was him and not her. In affairs of the heart a military gentleman of the nineteen-twenties had enormous problems. His head was filled with ideas of what was honourable and what was not. Unmarried officers were expected to associate with women only, as it were, at arm's length. Whores and Camp Followers were all very well for the other ranks but young Sir was supposed to be above that sort of thing. Womanizing before marriage was proscribed by the church, frowned on by the regiment and to all intents and purposes banned by King's Regulations. And young Air Force officers were not permitted to marry until they were thirty years old. On top of this, most military gentlemen had the feeling that they could offer a woman very little in a marriage bargain. They were poorly paid and always liable to be separated from loved ones. Their life expectancy, especially if they were flying Hyderabads by night, was acknowledged to be poor. So what could Flying Officer Ivelaw-Chapman do at the age of 29 when he was head over heels in love and bound by a code of honour and a powerful unselfishness to do nothing with his girlfriend that a chaperone would not approve of? Well, he could always apply for a posting to Baghdad.

CHAPTER 6

BAGHDAD TO JELLALABAD

Mesopotamia was part of the unfinished business that confronted the League of Nations at the end of the First World War. The land had been ruled by Turkey until the Ottoman Empire collapsed along with Imperial Germany in 1918. However, the country that lay between the Tigris and the Euphrates was a single nation in geography only. It was a hotchpotch of enemies, a lawless melting pot of Kurds and Turks, Sunni Moslems and Shi'ites interspersed with Jews and occupied by victorious European armies. The League of Nations decided that Mesopotamia should, on an instant, become Iraq; and Britain, as a victorious nation in the Great War, with a reputation of firm but fair rule in India, was given the mandate by the League to govern the whole volatile territory between the Rivers.

Iraq as a British Mandate was troublesome. There were Arab revolts, murders, assassinations. Iraqis, for all their racial diversity were united in their distaste for European Colonial rule. The British military commitment required to police the country grew and grew. Voices, notably those of T.E. Lawrence and Winston Churchill, were raised in protest against the wastage of life, limb and money in Iraq when it seemed that no material or strategic advantage could possibly accrue from our presence in Baghdad. So it was decided that if nothing was to be gained from the Mandate to govern Iraq, Iraq should without delay begin to govern itself. Feisal, a former rebel leader was made King after a plebiscite of dubious validity confirmed him as the Iraqi's choice. Thankfully the Mandate administrators bowed the knee to King Feisal and sailed for home leaving behind a small British military presence to police the vast areas of desert within the Kingdom, whose nomadic inhabitants were not quite sure who was in charge, and who didn't take kindly to anyone's authority.

Here at last was a serious fighting role for the aeroplane. A flying machine could move troops from barracks to outlying areas in hours as opposed to weeks. Policing of underdeveloped areas by aeroplane was a new concept and it was tried and tested for the first time in Iraq in the 1920s. Which is why there was an RAF base at Hinaidi, Baghdad in 1929, and why there were Vickers Victoria troop carriers based there and why there was a vacancy for a highly experienced twin-engined pilot by the name of Ivelaw-Chapman who, as a military man could in those days, had applied for a posting — to

51

anywhere in the world.

Biographical Notes. No 70 Squadron, Hinaidi.

The most interesting part of this tour was concerned with the Kabul evacuations which I shall describe later on.

But that does not mean that the rest of the time I spent with 70 Squadron was in any way dull. The Vickers Victoria was basically a troop carrier (It had seats for 22 persons) and we could also carry bombs. Most of our flying was over the featureless southern desert of Iraq where it was easy to lose one's bearings completely. Among other tasks, we used to carry personnel, rations and stores for the Desert Columns that were scattered about the area. I enjoyed most of all the occasions when our work entailed night stopping in the desert. After a stinking hot day it was amazing how soon and how low the temperature dropped after sundown. We always carried in our Victorias a large container of fresh water, a ration box of tinned foods of every variety and an ice box. We usually mustered some eight to ten of us (of all ranks) and as Captain of Aircraft I was in charge of the camp for the night and decided when and how much we should eat and drink. When the party was all over, I loved to sleep out in the desert under a starlit sky, possibly even under a blanket.

Once every 6 months we had the chance to do a Cairo run. We left Hinaidi at crack of dawn and flew across the desert to Transjordan. The route was fairly well defined by the fleet of Nairn motorcars that had worn visible tracks in the desert. Normally we put in at Rutbah Fort for refuelling and a bite of food half way across and then on to Amman for the night and Cairo the next morning. We were allowed 4 or 5 days to taste the delights of Cairo which were many and in great contrast to the austere existence that we led in Hinaidi. Personally I made a bee-line for two things; first a dinner at Jimmy's where they served a delicious prawn mayonnaise; and after that I loved to watch the game of Pelota Basque played by professionals either in Cairo or Alexandria.

We always had a long list of commissions to fulfil for individuals and messes. Heaven help the captain on a Cairo run who did not bring back a case of kippers for his Mess. One of our more colourful characters, Stewart Maxwell flew back from Cairo a Model T Ford which he had stripped down to components that would just go through the door of a Victoria.

Other tasks on the Squadron took me to Kuwait and Bandar Abbas on each side of the Persian Gulf. Northwards we had a regular run to Mosul, Diana and Rowanduz. On one Mosul run I brought back to Hinaidi among other things a goose for the Sergeants' Mess dinner and when we came to take it out of the cabin after the 3½ hour journey it had laid an egg. On

A Surprise from the Sky.

*. . . from the
cpit spun a
football."*

5. See p.28.

6. Betty Shortt ' ... you have seen your
future wife, you need look no further'
(p.40). Taken by her brother when she was
11.

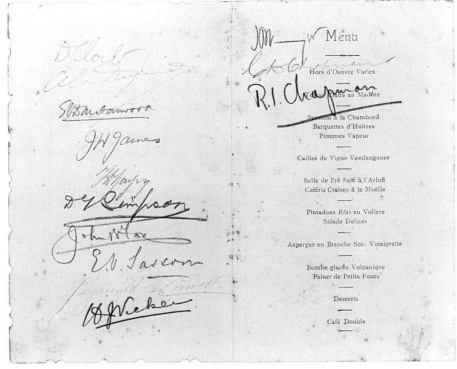

Menu

Hors d'Oeuvre Varies

Homard à la Chambord au Madère

Saumon à la Chambord
Barquettes d'Huîtres
Pommes Vapeur

Cailles de Vigne Vendangeuse

Selle de Prè Salé à l'Arloff
Celéris Craises à la Moëlle

Pintadons Rôti en Volière
Salade Delices

Asperges en Branche Sce. Vinaigrette

Bombe glacée Volcanique
Panier de Petits Fours

Desserts

Café Double

7. Menu from the Taj Hotel, Bombay. ' … the gymkhanas, the dances, the dinner parties, the picnics, the polo matches …' (p.31).

8. Airmail envelope of 1920.

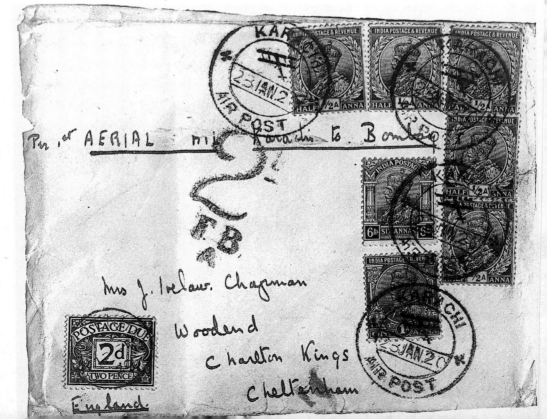

ROYAL AIR FORCE
AERIAL PAGEANT
HENDON
SATURDAY JUNE 30

9. It is determined to evacuate the post and destroy the bridge.' (p.43)

10. Martlesham Heath Dining-in Night menu.

MENU

SPRINGBOKS TAIL SOUP.

"GREBEN" DABS.
"ROE" SAUCE.

AWANA CHICKENS (SLOTTED WINGS)
"SISKIN" SAUSAGES.
"PIXIE" POTATOES. BRISTOL SPROUTS.

FAIREY MERINGUES.
BUGLE ECLAIRS.

WOODCOCK SAVOURY.
"34" CHEESE STRAWS.

VICTORIA DESSERT.

POMMARD.   SCOTCH WHISKY.
LIEBFRAUMILCH.   IRISH WHISKY.
BLACKBURNT COFFEE.

MARTLESHAM HEATH.
NOV. 2ND 1923.

11. 'The Parnall Possum, an aerodynamic non-starter' (p.42).

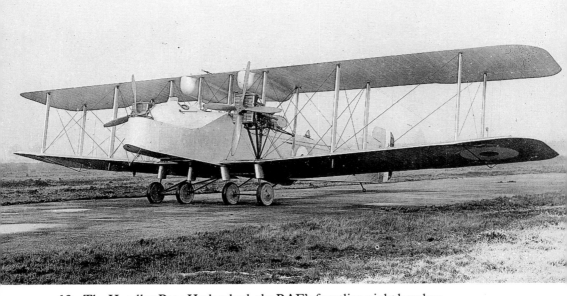

12. The Handley Page Hyderabad, the RAF's frontline night bomber in 1925.

13. Victoria en route to Kabul: 'The whole flight was carried out below safety height' (p.67).

another occasion I flew His Majesty King Feisal on a general tour of desert posts. I also flew to Baghdad Sheik Dawish who had been causing a lot of trouble in the Southern Desert.

Letters to his unofficial fiancée. Written 1929. Discovered 1990.

.....What was I doing at precisely 9pm British Summer Time or 11pm Baghdad local time on Wednesday June 13th? I'm afraid to say I was not in telepathic contact with you Dearest; I was sitting in an armchair in the Mess reading the Baghdad Times *with a whisky and soda in one hand and my pipe in the other and thinking of anything but Beckenham or England or you...sorry.*

Yes, Child, you get it into your head that I am going to be out here for eight years; then one day I'll walk through the gate of your house and surprise you.

> *Cheerioh; Thine for always and a day,*
> *ME.*

Hinaidi;
November 22nd

Darling Child,

I gloat, I gloat, I gloat; I have seen rain. The first since we came through the Straits of Gibraltar....

So you liked "The Ins and Outs of Mesopotamia"; it's quite an interesting book and gives you a real insight into the workings of that perplexing anomaly − the Eastern Mind...

> *God bless you always;*
> *Thine to the end,*
> *C*

Hinaidi;
11th July;
Good Morrow my Darling Good Morrow,

Come along Mutt [A wild dog from Baghdad that became his constant companion] *say good morning to the Missus. That's a good dog. Now then Mrs Chappie let's see if we can talk a little sense for two minutes...*

I went up to Mosul for a couple of days. That was very pleasant. I flew up on the Saturday − 220 miles before breakfast − complete with eight passengers besides my usual crew and Mutt. Mutt by the way is a most experienced aviator and has something over 500 flying hours to his credit. My passengers were a bunch of officers going up to the summer rest camp in the hills. *We fly them up as far as Mosul which is just at the foot of the hills. Then No 6 Squadron takes them on to an aerodrome one hundred miles further on and about 4000 feet up. Then they have a 2 days' march on mules till they eventually arrive at what from all accounts is a most delightful little summer camp, 8,500 feet up and tucked right away on the Persian border not much below the snow line. Personally I'm not going up for a spell this year — one can get a spell of 12 days if one feels one needs it.*

I didn't do anything very exciting at Mosul. In fact I didn't vary my usual daily programme at all. I slept in the afternoon, then tennis, supper, bridge as usual, both the days I was up there.

Coming back down on Monday was rather fun because there were low clouds completely obscuring the ground for the first 200 miles. I came down on a compass course without seeing the ground at all for over 2 hours on end and then to my surprise and delight I found I was dead on my track and exactly where I ought to have been. I got in here all right but it was so thick when I arrived one couldn't see across the aerodrome.

Since Monday we've had the usual round of squash, tennis, bridge, dining out etc. On Tuesday I dined with Tony Leach, late of Martlesham at 55 Squadron — they were having a guest night — and after dinner they ran a Roulette board out on their lawn. We didn't win a fortune... in fact we lost 5 chips so you won't be able to have the four wheel brakes on that scooter....

Bye Bye Beloved and God bless you
Thine more than ever,
Chappie.

The Continental-Savoy.
Cairo
November 29th 1928.
You Splendid Infant,
Every time I walk into a Mess I find another letter from you....

Now, where were we? I was just going off to Heliopolis; that was of course last Tuesday. Well, the last four days up here have been one hectic enjoyable dash round, seeing things, meeting people, spending money and dissipating generally. On the Tuesday I went down with a fellow called Tweedie to the Gegisa Club. It's a wonderful place where all the British Element meet. You can get every kind of sport here; tennis, hockey, polo, racing, squash, swimming, croquet, bowls, billiards etc. and it's always crammed with people. We played strenuous singles, had tea and a drink or two and then back to the camp; then back into Cairo where I had an honest-to-God fried sole and a steak and then back to bed earlyish. On Wednesday afternoon I went into Cairo and did a lot of shopping — working off a long list of commissions I had to fulfil for various people in Hinaidi. In the evening I went to see Pygmalion *at the Opera House done by an excellent British Company called the Robert Atkins. I loved it. Yesterday morning I visited the Egyptian Museum and spent most of my time in that section devoted to the recent acquisitions from the Tomb of Tutankhamun. That part was extraordinarily interesting and some of the exhibitions, particularly the old gentleman's actual coffin, fair take your breath away for sheer lavishness.*

In the evening I went down to Abassia barracks and collected Jack Boothby and we had a priceless evening together. We nibbled steak at Jimmy's and then saw Carter the Great Illusionist — I saw him before in Bombay last March. After that we went on to the Pelote Basque where we won 50 piastres each at the big game and then on to a cabaret.

You are a brick to send me all those letters to Egypt. It's wonderfully satisfying to go into a strange Mess in a strange country and find a letter waiting for you and when you find it's in the right handwriting it's not just satisfying...its er ...great. You are a good Pal you know. I must stop now because a. I must catch the post and b. I might wax sentimental in the smoking room of a Gyppie Hotel in broad daylight and the silent footed Sudanese servants wouldn't know what to make of that, would they?

God Bless you,
Thine for Ever,
C.

The Biographical Notes record the following three Anecdotes from Iraq. The stories need little introduction. They show Chaps as an enthusiastic adventurer, a young man who took real pleasure in the unusual experiences of his chosen career. He was clearly a romantic in the mould of T.E. Lawrence and more than a little in love with the desert and the wild Arab lands in which he was operating. The Bottle of Beaune story is quite significant because it defines the moment that he changed from a rather aimless, adventurous flier into an embryo strategist for whom high rank in the RAF was a real possibility. He always enjoyed the rather frivolous circumstances in which this important decision was taken.

Biographical Notes. Anecdotes. Buying Beer.

Whilst serving with No 70 Squadron in Iraq in 1929 I flew a spare engine to another pilot who had forced landed his Victoria in the desert. On these occasions the engine change normally involved 2 or 3 nights living out in the desert. With the crews of the two aircraft, plus the engine-changing mechanics, the ration strength on the spot often rose to 10 or even 12. Each aircraft had its own ration box and extra rations were carried for these special occasions. But by the third evening our party was getting desperately short of beer. It so happened that this forced landing had taken place close to the single-track railway line laid across the 300 miles of desert separating Basra from Baghdad. A passenger train was scheduled along this line in each direction once during every 24 hours and I happened to know that the northbound train was due to pass at about 9pm. So three of us, armed with a Very pistol and a box of cartridges, hiked to the railway line and awaited the 'Express' which actually travelled very slowly. One could see its approach from miles away and as it drew close we fired across its path with everything we'd got. The driver stopped the train in a cloud of steam. He was a bit agitated, but he soon calmed down when he discovered that all we wanted was a case of beer, on repayment, from his restaurant car.

Biographical Notes. Anecdotes. Ancient and Modern.

In 1928 while serving with No 70 Squadron in Iraq I was sent off with my Victoria to a camp at Ur, 6 miles west of Nasiriyah in the southern desert of Iraq. Our job was to fly out from there a couple of hundred miles into the desert keeping in contact with various mobile columns of armoured cars and Iraqi Levies who were attempting to uphold law and order amongst tribesmen who refused allegiance to the King of Iraq. At this camp, which was codenamed Urcol, we had an up-to-date landing ground, modern aeroplanes, radio communication with Baghdad and the rest of the world. We lived a reasonably civilized life in tents, ate tinned European food and had ice to cool our drinks. We played bridge and listened to broadcasts from Europe.

By contrast if we walked half a mile to the north of our camp we entered an area where, under the direction of Sir Leonard Woolley, excavations were afoot into a civilization dating back to at least 2500 BC, and in a spot reputed to have been the birthplace of Abraham. Even though our equipment was quite primitive, we could still get a radio message to London in the twinkling of an eye and our flying machines could transport us to Egypt in a day and the land of Canaan in a few hours. The contrast with the archaeology of biblical and prehistoric life that was being uncovered so near to our camp was quite arresting.

He sent a postcard to England from this camp. It was datelined, Ur of the Chaldees, Friday and contained the immortal line; "Having a wonderful time; wish you were Ur."

Biographical Notes. Anecdotes: A Bottle of Beaune and its Consequences.

Round about 1928 I was serving with No 70 Squadron at Hinaidi in Iraq and 'Dolly' Gray was with 55 Squadron at the same station. Although we had separate Messes, Dolly and I had an arrangement whereby on most Saturday evenings, if we were not away on Ops, we would have dinner together in one of the restaurants in Baghdad where they maintained a semblance of European cuisine.

On one such occasion he and I did a little bit of heart searching. We were both aged about 29 with 10 or 12 years' service behind us; very junior Flight Lieutenants, me at any rate with the hope of marriage at the end of my tour yet we had no serious prospects either in or out of the Service. We could both fly reasonably well and had plenty of experience in a variety of types of aircraft. But apart from that we had nothing to show for ourselves.

To get on in the service one either had to specialize by taking a course in engineering, armament, photography or something similar or to qualify as a staff officer by attending the RAF Staff College at Andover. The first alternative did not appeal to either of us and we both seriously doubted our mental capacity to tackle the second. It so happened that the names of junior officers who had been successful in the Staff College qualifying exam had been recently published in Air Ministry Weekly Orders. Under the influence of the bottle of Beaune, Dolly and I began to convince ourselves that we were potential staff officers. This we achieved largely by comparing our own intellectual abilities, an assessment suitably optimized by the intake of good wine, with various blockheads of our acquaintance who seemed to have passed the qualifying exam satisfactorily. We then ordered a second bottle and promised each other that the next Monday morning, without fail, we would go to our respective commanding officers and apply to sit the next Staff College qualifying exam. This we did, and by the following Saturday we were doing our level best to get out of it. Hinaidi was too hot for swotting; the recommended study list struck terror into the pair of us; there was serious flying to be done, dinners to be eaten at Jimmy's in Cairo. However, our attempts to retract were rejected by the AOC Middle East.

So Dolly and I gave up our Saturday night revelry and devoted our spare time to the exam; we studied form and mugged up alternate subjects, getting together later to brief each other on what we had mastered. We applied the law of probabilities and wasted no time on subjects that came up only infrequently. Four months later we sat the exam; I passed and Dolly had to resit one subject only.

It was not possible in the peacetime RAF for an officer to earn promotion to Air rank without graduating from the RAF Staff College. In other words officers could never 'Fly their way to the top'. Sooner or later a man had to make a conscious decision to hang up his flying boots and study if he was going to climb out of the mass of highly qualified aviators of which the RAF is never short. It was in that restaurant in Baghdad that Chaps and Dolly Gray made this decision and they never regretted it. Nor should those who benefited from their wisdom and personality as Air Marshals in later years.

Dolly Gray's partial failure of the Staff College qualifying exam was due, largely, to the facetious answer he gave to a question on naval strategy. "What," he was asked, "is your opinion of the military value of the aircraft carrier?" Dolly Gray, who was no mean cartoonist, answered this by drawing a picture of an ungainly, topheavy flat-top with biplane fighters falling off its flight deck into the sea. "Military value of the aircraft carrier?" he wrote, "Well just look at the bloody thing."

The late J.A. Gray was a Group Captain at the start of the Second World War and won the George Medal while serving as Station Commander, RAF Honnington. At the height of the Bomber Offensive he was Senior Air Staff Officer Bomber Command where he was Bomber Harris's closest adviser and responsible for some of the most difficult "Go or No-Go" decisions that were made before the great bomber raids on Germany.

If they hadn't taken a glass or two too many of Beaune in a Baghdad restaurant in 1929 both Dolly Gray and Chaps would probably have been out of the RAF by 1940. They would have pleaded for recall and maybe served out the war in the Royal Observer Corps or perhaps as comparatively elderly flying instructors at one of the Empire flying schools.

Long after his retirement from the RAF Chaps happily acknowledged his debt to this particular Burgundy. Beaune was always in the picnic hamper at Glyndebourne; it was drunk at most family celebrations and at the grander dinner parties. The wine waiter in the RAF Club produced a bottle unasked whenever Sir Ronald was dining in the restaurant. "I got in trouble with this stuff in Baghdad in '29," he would say, "and I still love it."

And that's how we find him in Iraq at the end of the 1920s. In some ways he was at the top of his profession. Any limitations that he once may have had as a pilot were cancelled out by experience. There was now no better man in a Victoria than Flight Lieutenant Ivelaw-Chapman and he had probably flown everywhere in the Middle East where an aeroplane could go to. He had lots of friends in Baghdad and in Cairo and he was sustaining by letter his love affair with Margaret, his unofficial fiancée. The Staff College qualifying exam was behind him, and marriage and probably promotion were awaiting him when his tour with 70 Squadron ended and he came home once more. And then the word came from Kabul...

Biographical Notes. The Kabul Air Evacuations, 1929.

The Kabul Air Evacuations of 1929 played an important part in my Service life. I learnt a lot from the relatively minor part that I played in those operations and I gained an unwarrantable amount of kudos.

At the tail end of 1928 the city of Kabul in Afghanistan lay between two opposing armies fighting a violent Civil War for possession of the city. The scene of some of the bloodiest battles in this war was that part of the city where the British Legation was situated. The British Minister there, Sir Francis Humphrys, called upon the Government of India for the evacuation by air of all British and Indian women and children from the Legation. Consequently a number of Victorias from No 70 Squadron in Iraq, which was the nearest transport squadron, were summoned from Baghdad to Risalpur in the North-West Frontier Province of India to undertake this airlift from Kabul.

I was lucky enough to be among those selected for this task but unfortunately I was held up at Karachi for an engine change en route. By the time I reached Risalpur the evacuation of the women and children had been completed and our small detachment of Victorias was standing by in case Sir Francis Humphrys called for a complete evacuation of his and all European Legations in the City.

He doesn't make much of the flight to India but it was something of an epic in itself. There is a long letter to his fiancée from Karachi that shows the sheer excitement of piloting an aircraft along a route that was virtually unknown and the memories of an airman who supervised the refuelling at a staging post along the way shows what remarkably sophisticated logistical back-up the RAF could call on even in 1928.

Letter to Margaret dated 29/12/28.

RAF Depot − Drigh Road
Karachi. Saturday.
Darling Che − ild
Well here we are back in India again having fulfilled one of my long-cherished ambitions. I've flown the length of the Persian Gulf. The story begins about a week ago. I was told to get all ready to move off at dawn on Monday 24th December with Karachi as my first destination, and after that I'd come under the command of AOC India for further movements. Sunday was spent in a general flap. The biggest trouble was to get our ten passports (Two machines − five people in each) duly visa-ed for Persia on a Sunday morning in Baghdad when everybody was away at the beginning

of the Christmas holidays. However, after a lot of chasing around I managed to get them delivered at Hinaidi by 6pm. During the afternoon I managed to fit in a game of hockey and the evening was spent in final arrangements such as extra food on the machine including a tinned plum pudding and several steak and kidney pies for our Christmas dinner. I got to bed elevenish, was up by 5.30, had a spot of breakfast and got off the ground by 7.45 and set off South with a very favourable wind. We made the first 300 miles to Shaibah in exactly 3 hours and landed to refuel. We took in about 300 gallons of fuel each, had a spot of tiffin with 84 Squadron, and off again about 1pm. From then on I was over new country to me as we crossed the Iraq/Persia frontier just outside Basra. The first 60-odd miles was over the marshlands and delta of the combined Tigris and Euphrates with the deep blue of the Persian Gulf away to the South. I did another 245 miles to my first port of call on the Gulf at Bushire where we fetched up about 4pm. We found the Anglo-Persian Oil Company people awaiting us with 600 gallons of petrol which we put in while I battled with the Customs, Military, Passport and Civil authorities. Conversation was difficult and varied between French, Hindustani, pidgin English and a spot of Arabic.

We got both machines ready for the morning and then lit a camp fire and got down to a hearty meal of bacon, sausages, tea, beer and biscuits. It was a perfect night (Christmas Eve); practically full moon and I slept outside on a camp bed and the troops slept in the machines. First day completed according to programme; 550 miles in 6 hours flying. I was up first the next morning about two hours before dawn (Christmas morning) and having wished you a happy Christmas I turned out the crews of the two machines who soon got a fire going and we had cocoa and biscuits before taking off just before sunrise.

We were in the air exactly 5 hours and covered 422 miles to Bandar Abbas. We followed the coast line more or less the whole way and a more desolate, inhospitable and barren shore I never wish to see; mile upon mile of lava rock where the foothills of enormous mountain ranges merge into the rocky cliffs of the coast itself. Incidentally as we went eastward so it got warmer and warmer and we lost more and more daylight.

We landed at Bandar Abbas about noon on Christmas day and I did battle once again with the passport and immigration authorities. The British Consul there invited us to go along to the Consulate and take tiffin with him and a very welcome glass of iced lager; there were two or three other Britishers there and we quite caught the Christmas atmosphere. We were off the ground again by 2pm heading for Jask, another 170 miles down the coast which I hoped to make well before dark. It was just after I'd got in the air that afternoon that the miracle happened. My wireless operator passed *me up a message he had just received from all of you at Cheltenham. I was just over the most desolate piece of coastline when I got the message and I can tell you it fair warmed the cockles of me 'art; and do you know how they reached me? The message arrived by ordinary civil Cable at the Squadron at Baghdad, the Squadron sent it on by Service wireless to Shaibah who relayed it to a naval Persian Gulf sloop lying off the island of Henjam who relayed it on to me in the air. Pretty good eh, to get a private cable in the air on Christmas afternoon half way between Bandar Abbas and Jask about 4 o'clock in the evening.*

We got into Jask about 5pm. I went to work, by moonlight, on a defect on one of my engines with my fitter and I set my second pilot on to preparing our Christmas fare for the evening. We got down to it about 9pm and I don't think I've ever enjoyed a Christmas evening more. We were filthy dirty because we couldn't afford any water to wash or shave with and we sat in the open. Jask is a "Place" that's all; not any sort of town. By moonlight we devoured the steak and kidney pie, plum pudding and fruit and biscuits. I produced a bottle of whisky and one of rum from my personal ration box and we boiled a kettle on the camp fire to make a rum punch. We all got a little drunk.

I turned the troops in to bed about 11 and made up my camp bed alongside the machine, but the moon over the sea was too good to miss so I strolled up and down for an hour along the shore by myself, thinking of this and that and of Cheltenham and you and it was good.

He was entitled to feel good. It was Christmas night and he'd had a cable from home. He was leading a group on its way to a great adventure and the dinner party on the desert airstrip by the sea must have combined the appeal of a barbecue with the youthful comradeship of a Scout Camp. The lads would have loved the two bottles of liquor magically produced at the critical moment from the Captain's goody box; a classic leadership gesture this, copied, no doubt, from Napier John Gill. But the lion's share of his euphoria must have come from a sense of achievement. We should look a little deeper into the difficulties of completing a pioneering flight such as this. The commander of a primitive aeroplane flying an unfamiliar route literally drove himself, his crew and his machine to its destination, overcoming difficulties by sheer force of personality. We get a glimpse from the letter of the administrative problems that could have delayed him. Another couple of iced lagers with the British Consul at Bandar Abbas and they might have found an excuse to abandon their schedule in favour of Christmas hospitality, and when they finally arrived at Jask the faulty engine had to be worked on by a fitter and the detachment commander himself before there was any relaxation. But Chaps knew that the aircraft were needed in India, and nothing was to be allowed to slow them down.

Aeroplanes today do not fall out of the sky if they lose the power of one of their engines. In 1929 they did. The Victoria simply did not fly on one engine; there was too much drag and not enough thrust. So for every minute of these five-hour legs the pilots would have been listening above the eighty-knot slipstream howling past the open cockpits for the first irregularity in the steady beat of the twin Napier Lions driving the great wooden propellers (fixed pitch — non-feathering) that were thrashing round out on the wings. If one of them failed during the heat of the day, and he tells us that it was getting hotter as they flew East, there was probably two minutes' gliding time before a crash landing. They carried no parachutes and no dinghies or life-saving jackets. The coast was hostile and desolate with lava cliffs extending into the unfriendly sea. A forced landing was out of the question. Small wonder that they found cause for celebration in their safe arrival at each landing ground and he can be forgiven for feeling a little pleased with himself as he strode along the beach at Jask in the moonlight that Christmas night in 1928.

No one had fallen out of the sky... yet.

Before sunrise the next morning they were off again bound for Karachi. En route they refuelled at a God-forsaken airstrip at Pasni in Baluchistan where they took on the required 350 gallons of petrol/Benzol mixture. How the fuel got to Pasni was itself something of an epic.

The following account is reprinted from Anne Baker's book *Wings over Kabul* which she wrote in partnership with Sir R. Ivelaw-Chapman in 1975. The story is told by an airman who was stationed at Karachi at the time.

"On the 23rd December, 1928, when I was stationed at the RAF Depot at Drigh Road, Karachi, I was ordered to supervise the movement of 1000 gallons of petrol in a barge to a small village called Pasni 250 miles up the coast of Baluchistan from Karachi. About ten miles inland from the village there was an emergency landing strip and that was the destination for the 1000 gallons which was all in five gallon drums. We sailed from Karachi in an Indian Marine tugboat that was towing a fuel barge and arrived at Pasni about 0300 hrs on Boxing Day. We had to anchor offshore and as there was no jetty the fuel had to be carried ashore by natives. After a few hours' sleep at the home of the local agent for the British India Line we were awakened and given tea (Indian style — sweet but no milk) and then we supervised the loading of the petrol drums on to camels for the ten-mile journey to the landing strip. Later we were provided with a camel each and a mounted armed escort. This was my very first camel ride and the whole adventure thrilled and excited me. The camels were of the 'Trotting' variety and I don't recommend them as a comfortable means of transport.

When we got to the landing strip we found the petrol had already been unloaded so all we had to do was to await the arrival of the Victorias. During this wait in very hot sun I was offered what was to be my first and last 'Chapatti'. Having had nothing to eat but some bully beef and biscuits on Christmas day I did feel the need for some food. But the 'Chapatti', the camel ride and the hot sun were all too much for me and I was still vomiting when I heard the sound of the first Victoria in the distance. When they landed the crew disembarked and started overwing refuelling by hand pump from the drums. The pilot introduced himself to me. His name was Flight Lieutenant Ivelaw-Chapman.''

Napier John Gill please note: the airman who wrote this account was suffering from either food poisoning or sunstroke when he met Chaps briefly on a desert airstrip in Baluchistan in 1928. He seems to have had no problem recalling the rather complicated surname of the detachment commander even after a time lapse of around 50 years.

Letter to his fiancée. Drigh Road, 29th December 1928.

The next morning after an early breakfast of cocoa and cheese we were off again before sunrise on our last leg of 600 miles. About 200 miles along the coast we passed the Persian/Indian frontier at Gwattar and I was devoutly thankful to be flying over British soil again. We landed at Pasni in British India some 4½ hours after leaving Jask. There we found two airmen waiting for us who had been sent out from Karachi with fuel. On the last 245 miles to Karachi I cut the corner a bit and flew the last eighty or ninety miles over the sea and we landed at Karachi about 4.30 in the evening dead on schedule. We were pretty tired all round and filthy dirty. I hadn't been out of my clothes since I left Baghdad and hadn't washed or shaved.

I really don't know what the job is that we're here for nor have I an idea how long it will last. I believe it is something to do with the trouble in Kabul and I'm hoping it may entail a visit to that city, the capital of Afghanistan.

It's awful fun being back here again in India (I was stationed here in Karachi in December, 1919) and talking Hindustani and all that sort of thing and I can see I'm going to enjoy myself.

Well, beloved, I am sending this by the Persian Gulf mail boat to Basra and thence by Air Mail to Cairo so with any luck it ought to reach you a fortnight next Monday, that's the 14th.

You know as well as I do that all this travelling around doesn't perturb me in the slightest and my thoughts are with you just the same as soon as the tension and excitements of the day are over and I can be left alone with my thoughts...sounds like a cheap novel!

Cheerioh and God bless you
Thine eternally,
C.

His destination was, as he imagined, Kabul. After a frustrating 10-day wait in Karachi he set off for Risalpur in much the same state of mind as he was when awaiting call-up for the First World War. He was concerned that the drama would not last long enough for him to take part in it. He need not have worried.

The book *Wings over Kabul* describes in detail the build-up to Sir Francis Humphrys' appeal for the air evacuation of British citizens from the embattled legation in Afghanistan's capital. The situation was desperate and the beleaguered British were conducting themselves, while in extreme danger, with the gallantry and resolve that typified this generation.

Wings over Kabul. Chapter 6: Crisis in Kabul.
Quote from Sir Francis Humphrys, the British Minister in Kabul.

"We have all had charmed lives. My house looks like a radiator in places. Between the two windows of my upstairs study there are 40 bullet holes. None came through the window in front of which I was constantly moving. On the other hand many came through my bathroom window, one hitting my shaving glass and singeing my moustache; while a shell missed my head by nine inches and lodged in the wall. Others had more hairy experiences. A lot of VC work was done outside. All my staff behaved magnificently."

On 18 December Lady Humphrys wrote:

"Heavy shelling...very disturbing to the Minister's ablutions. Hospital hit; operating theatre's plate-glass windows smashed. A wounded man found in the kitchen."

Sir Geoffrey Salmond wrote:

"The only remaining means of communication with the British Legation through the Afghan wireless ceased abruptly during the transmission of an urgent message from Sir Francis Humphrys. This was to the effect that he wished to evacuate the women and children of the legation as soon as possible and requested a reconnaissance aeroplane to be sent up to Kabul."

Anne Baker continues: "This signal was received at 9.55am on 17th December. It was confirmed at 1715 at Quetta on December 17th. This confirmation was due to the skill and foresight of Sir Francis himself. While on home leave in 1927 he went into a West End shop and bought the compact wireless set which had been displayed in the window. When he realized that he could no longer use the Afghan wireless on 17 December he slung his aerial to a tree outside the window of the Legation and tapped out an experimental SOS on his set. To his amazement the message was picked up in Quetta and confirmed the earlier request.

"His call for help was passed by Sir Geoffrey Salmond to Sir Dennis Bray and by him to Sir Samuel Hoare. On 18 December Sir Geoffrey was empowered to ask for as many Victorias as he felt necessary from Sir Robert Brooke-Popham in Baghdad. He had the blessing of Whitehall and, even more important to him, the tremendous support and encouragement from Sir Hugh Trenchard.

"Meanwhile the white sheets spelling out the message for the first reconnaissance aircraft from India, DO NOT LAND, FLY HIGH ALL'S WELL, lay out on the grass in the moonlight and from time to time Sir Francis and Lady Humphrys and those anxious men and women in the Legation would glance through the shattered windows at the grey mountains between themselves and Peshawar and safety, and wonder if their messages had got through and if an aeroplane would come."

Everything was going to be all right. With the earnest support of all those Knights and the driving enthusiasm of the CO of 70 Squadron in Baghdad plus the personal endeavours of Flight Lieutenant Ivelaw-Chapman and his colleagues, how could the aeroplanes fail to arrive?

We should consider for a moment why an air evacuation of the British in Kabul was vital. Not only were there hordes of murderous Afghan tribesmen milling around the gates of the beleaguered British Legation, two hundred years of bloodstained history were making themselves felt as well. There are said to be a thousand British dead for every mile of the Khyber road that joins the North West Frontier province of India to the Kabul plain. In the first Afghan war a retreating column of 16,000 rank and file were wiped out between Kabul and Jellalabad half way down the Road. In the Second, the gates of the British Residency were stormed and every living soul inside was put to the sword. The very name Kabul struck terror into the hearts of the British military. So even in 1929 it was out of the question for a small British community to retreat through a hostile Khyber Pass on foot, and a relieving column from India would never have risked a third Afghan massacre by marching once again into the unforgiving mountains.

Chaps, belatedly winging his way from Karachi to Risalpur, knew all about Kabul and the Khyber. He was probably carrying in his baggage a sun-faded leather-bound copy of Kipling's verse that went with him on most journeys. The flyleaf was inscribed "Chaps from Tony. 17th January 1922. Risalpur North West Frontier Province India." That was of course Tony Shortt, the close companion of his earlier time in India, the 'David and Jonathan' friend of the great Himalayan Trek who was now only one year away from becoming Chaps' brother-in-law. Two poems were probably already committed to Chaps' memory.

"Kabul town's by Kabul river
Blow the bugle, draw the sword
There I left my mate for ever,
Wet and dripping by the ford."

And the bloodthirsty stanza from 'The Young British Soldier' that is used to set the scene in the early chapters of *Wings over Kabul* is one that Chaps often quoted:

"When you're wounded and left on Afghanistan's plains
And the women come out to cut up what remains,
Just roll to your rifle and blow out your brains
And go to your Gawd like a soldier."

He could be forgiven for enormous frustration during the ten days that he was forced to wait on the ground at Karachi. All his efforts to hustle his machine and crew from Baghdad in the shortest possible time were negated by engine failure on arrival. The replacement Napier Lion had to come from his home base by sea and by the time it arrived the greater part of the evacuation of the women and children from Kabul had been successfully completed. However in spite of the added difficulties caused by the doubtful performance of the replacement engine he finally made it to Peshawar and there was still plenty of work to be done.

Wings Over Kabul. Chapter 11: No 70 Squadron RAF.

On referring to my log book I find that on January 11th 1929 on my way to Risalpur from Karachi (just after I had had a new engine installed there) I had only been in the air 55 minutes before I forced landed in the Lakki Hills by reason of overheating. The fitter in my crew must have fixed that pretty smartly as I see we were in the air 40 minutes later, but only to forced land again after an hour and a quarter at Pad Idan — presumably an emergency airstrip — to change a propeller. This was effected in one hour and forty minutes and we were airborne again shortly after 11am. We got though to Lahore that evening just before the sun went down.

By the time I reached Risalpur the evacuation of the women and children had been completed and our small detachment of Victorias was standing by in case Sir Francis Humphrys called for a complete evacuation of all the Europeans in the city.

During this "Standby" a special mission arose, namely to fly out the reigning King of Afghanistan, Inayatullah. The previous King, Amanullah, had fled to Kandahar at the height of the rebellion, but before leaving had persuaded his brother, Inayatullah, to accept, very reluctantly, the throne. Inayatullah was a weak character and after a reign of only three and a half days Sir Francis realized that the King's presence in Kabul was aggravating an already ticklish situation in the city. Accordingly on January 18th Maxwell and I in our respective Victorias went into Kabul to fly out this King of 3½ days with his entire entourage. I evacuated the King plus a few followers and Maxwell took some part of the harem of wives and concubines.

I should describe the nature of the flight between Risalpur and Sherpur, the airfield on the outskirts of Kabul. For the first 40 miles we were slowly climbing over the rather dull and featureless plain that constitutes the northwest corner of the NWFP of India with Peshawar just visible to the south of our track. By the time we drew level with the Khyber Pass the scenery changed as we entered the lower ranges of the Hindu Kush massif. We had not had time by then to reach our maximum height so we had to thread our way through the valleys sometimes twisting in our tracks to conform with the run of the valley below us. From then on ragged mountains towered above us on both sides, some rising to 9 or 10 thousand feet. On most occasions these higher peaks were snow-covered which added to the grandeur of the panoramic view but was in deep contrast to the blackness of the narrow gorges and valleys immediately below us. After about an hour of this we approached the Latoband Pass which lies between two peaks rising up to some 10,000 feet, that looked like sentinels guarding the Pass. Once through the Pass the ground below began to level off slightly as we debouched on to the Kabul Plain (itself 6,000 feet above sea level) with the Kabul River winding its way through the middle and producing welcome signs of vegetation and human habitation for the last 30 miles of our journey. The return flight from Kabul to Peshawar produced even more magnificent scenery since our track lay slightly to the south of our outward run. It took us over mountain scenery almost continuously and ended with a splendid view of the Khyber Pass with the picturesque and historic road winding its way through from Loe Dakka in Afghanistan to Landi Kotal and thence into India.

We can be sure that the terrain was beautiful and the mountains quite majestic as they thrust upwards to the snow line and beyond. They were also lethal and the realities of the Kabul run in a Victoria were such that no modern aviator would have considered it. The whole flight was carried out below safety height. This means that the pilots could not keep clear of the peaks by flying above the mountains; they were forced by reason of the aircraft's performance to fly around them. They flew down the valleys and darted between the crests and depended upon visual clearance to avoid crashing into the towering rock-piles of the Khyber. But what happened when clouds obscured the peaks, when snow flurries blotted out the pilot's forward visibility, when the way into a valley was clear but the way out was obscured? No pilot on the evacuation ever turned back because of the weather. Brave to a fault, they forced their machines through the Pass; half-frozen in their open cockpits and navigating by an uncanny sense of direction they got through to Kabul and completed the evacuation — all except one.

Biographical Notes. Service Memories.

On my next flight I was due to fly out some of the Legation staff but in fact I never reached Kabul. With Davies as my second pilot and with a completely empty and stripped Victoria I was flying west at 12,000 ft over some dirty mountainous country when, as the snow-covered Kabul plain came into sight in the far distance, first one and immediately the other of my two engines faded. Nothing that I could do would get them going again. Losing height, I turned off course towards the Kabul River in the hope of finding some less forbidding terrain than that immediately below me. But long before I caught sight of the river I realized that I should have to land somewhere pretty soon. I spotted a piece of ground a mile or so ahead which looked slightly less precipitous than its surrounds and I headed for it. As I glided towards it I saw that it was far from flat and boulder strewn. But I had no engine power; I was losing height rapidly and to smash into the rocky side of a mountain was the only alternative. I decided to have a go.

Now was the time to recall the hard-learned lessons of flying training, the practice engine failures, the simulated forced landings, the hazardous power-off approaches into fields around Grantham. Remember the instructor's words bellowed down Gosport tubes and crackling through rudimentary intercoms: "Nose down, Chapman, trim into the glide, pick a landing point, check for cause of failure, err on the high side, never stretch a glide, lower flap, never lift it, side slip if desperate, look out for cows/sheep/camels/boulders/trees ... not bad Chapman, round we go again."

Biographical Notes. Kabul Air Evacuations 1929. Continued.

As I came up to my selected Forced Landing Ground I found I had to sideslip off my remaining height if I was not going to overrun this tiny plateau which was only about 60 yards long and less in breadth. On three sides it dropped away steeply for a couple of hundred feet. Having got into about the right position I stalled my Victoria from a height of about 10 feet deliberately losing all flying speed so that the aeroplane would drop to the ground by its own weight and more or less stay put where it arrived. The impact of course broke the undercarriage and stove in the underbelly of the fuselage, but did us no more damage than to bruise Davies' knee rather badly. We were very lucky.

He got it right. There are those who say that aviation is 90% boredom and 10% sheer panic, and it is during that last 10% that a pilot earns his money. Chaps certainly earned his during those few moments when he found himself totally without power over an intensely hostile terrain. But, having survived the forced landing, what sort of reception could the two pilots expect from the tribesmen on the ground, from the bloodthirsty men of the Khyber who had been systematically butchering the British army for the last 200 years?

"When you're wounded and left on Afghanistan's plains...."

Biographical Notes. Kabul Air Evacuations 1929. Continued.

From the air we had not seen a soul, but we were soon surrounded by a mob of heavily armed and wildly shouting Afghan tribesmen. They were speaking in Pushtu which neither of us understood. I produced my 'Blood Chit' and handed it round, but they couldn't read, so pandemonium reigned. After about 20 minutes a gentleman wearing a military overcoat arrived and quietened down the tribesmen. He belonged to a rebel faction that supported Ali Ahmed Khan and was himself a Brigadier. His attitude to us was not hostile but he was obviously sceptical about our 'Blood Chits'. This was because he and his countrymen had, from time immemorial, associated British soldiers with khaki uniform. Because it was midwinter, Davies and I were wearing RAF blue tunics and this was the reason for their uncertainty. Some Russian pilots, wearing a similar blue uniform, had recently indulged in some pretty promiscuous bombing in Afghanistan and they were definitely not popular with the tribesmen. It wasn't surprising that he needed a lot of convincing, in my limited Urdu, of the peaceful nature of our mission. Nevertheless he was quite correct in his procedure and posted sentries on the wrecked machine. He then led us off down the mountainside to a neighbouring village where we were given green tea and chapattis. The Afghan Brigadier then sent off, by mounted messenger, a letter concerning us to some unknown destination. That night we spent crammed together with a dozen evil-smelling tribesmen and a charcoal fire in a small farm building with no ventilation.

During the night I kept turning over in my mind possible reasons for both of my engines failing at practically the same moment. Admittedly in those days engine reliability was not what it is today and failure of a single engine was not altogether unknown, but to lose both within seconds of each other was surprising. I surmised that it must have been due in some way to petrol flow but that was difficult to believe because each engine had its independent supply. At any rate I was determined to get to know the reason if I possibly could. Accordingly at dawn the next morning I persuaded our Brigadier friend to take me back up the hill to the crashed Victoria where I took out the petrol filters from both engines. The Napier Lion engines ran on petrol/ benzol mix which was not in common use by the RAF in India. The drums from which we refuelled had been in storage for a long time and condensation had gathered in the benzol. Throughout the flight from Peshawar water had been building up in the fuel filters of both engines and in the bitter cold at 10,000 feet en route to Kabul ice had formed and blocked the flow. It had never unfrozen and when I removed the filters they were still blocked with ice; dramatic evidence of the cause of our crash.

I could also see that the machine, even if it could be repaired, would never be flown off the rocky plateau on which I had perched it.

We went back to the village where a reply had now arrived to the Brigadier's message of the previous day. It was, of course, in Pushtu but a postscript at the bottom read, "Please come to Ali Ahmed Khan and be satisfied." Cryptic though that message was, I realized that if ever we reached the sender we should at last be able to communicate with some one in our own language. I was very glad, therefore, to see ponies being saddled and a short time later Davies and I set off on horseback with an escort of 12 heavily armed Afghans.

For 25 miles or more we marched along rough tracks mainly covered in snow, crossed frozen rivers and climbed steep gradients in a piercingly bitter wind. We reached the camp of General Ali Ahmed Khan well after nightfall and were put into a small rest house at Jagdallak that the General was using as his headquarters. Here we spent 6 days being held strictly as political prisoners. Davies, who by nature was somewhat morose, passed much of the time humming hymn tunes or lying on his bed staring vacantly at the ceiling. For him the world seemed to have come to an end. To stir him from this mental attitude I composed crossword puzzles and arithmetical problems and offered them to him for solution, but with only partial success. I was more successful when I improvised a draught board using matches as pieces and we passed many an hour in this way. One evening the monotony of our sojourn was relieved when the walls of our little room began to tilt and I realized we were having a small earthquake. The sentry at our door fled and we joined him in the open pretty rapidly.

On the fourth day of our stay at Jagdallak, a Sowar, a fine specimen of Shinwari manhood, arrived on foot to greet us. He was one of 20 Sowars sent out by the British political agent in the Khyber Pass to search for us. On the next day another Afghan walked in from Kabul with a letter, some fruit and cigarettes from Sir Francis Humphrys, the British Minister still under threat in his Legation in Kabul. Soon after, for the first time we were taken into the presence of the General. He told us that he had made arrangements to get us through by road to India since he could not guarantee the safety of the road between him and Kabul. He gave me despatches addressed to the Chief Commissioner at Peshawar and another addressed to the Viceroy of India. He also presented our Shinwari Sowar with a Mauser automatic. These formalities over we set off accompanied by an armed guard in a decrepit Chevrolet van bound for Jellalabad on the road towards India.

Throughout the day we were frequently stopped by small gangs of tribesmen wanting to know our business. Late in the afternoon things took rather an ugly turn when we were held up by a couple of hundred armed men who were quite obviously opposed to our sponsor General Ali Ahmed Khan. They shouted at and harangued our escort for an hour or more and I surmise that it was only our presence that prevented a battle. How the argument was settled I never knew but eventually we got under way again, but this time accompanied by several of this latest band who were obviously seeking reward for our safe conduct through their territory. The Chevrolet, designed to carry 12, now held 23 and the rest of journey was slow, smelly and precarious.

Very late that evening we reached the British Consulate in Jellalabad only to find that our Consul there had been forced to flee the town when the rebellion was at its height. He himself was now a refugee under the protection of a remarkable man known as the Pir Sahib of Baghdad who lived in a fort about 8 miles away. We drove to this Fort and were made welcome by the Consul and the Pir Sahib's entourage.

It is hard not to feel envy when reading this story. In the 1990s we are nostalgic for a forgotten way of life when such adventures were commonplace. We constantly try to recapture the drama and excitement that was freely available to young Britons in the 1920s in the course of their daily lives as servants of the British Empire. But there was a price that they had to pay. Men like Chaps built their lives on the principle of unquestioning service to the Crown; they personified the excellence of the British Way of Life. Sadly they were not quite able, 30 years later, to cope with the inevitable decline of the Empire. When the British Way became, by comparison with the Old Days, second rate, the Edwardian Military Gentlemen took it almost as a personal affront and their views on international affairs and politics were always coloured by the memory of the way things used to be.

Let us consider for a moment the wider implications of the situation in which Chaps and his co-pilot found themselves after the machine crashed in the mountains. How did they survive the first few moments of confrontation with the "hostile, heavily armed and wildly shouting Afghan tribesmen"? They weren't put to the sword on the spot because of the possibility, later to be confirmed, that they were British. Even in Afghanistan the superior military strength of the British Empire meant that swift retribution could be expected to follow any unprovoked attack on the forces of the Crown.

In 1929 an Englishman abroad, however youthful, had about him an unmistakable air of command. It was as though the omnipotence of the Empire made itself felt in the demeanour of its operatives all over the world. We read of subalterns barely out of their teens quelling an angry mob by standing firm and reading the Riot Act in a voice that betrayed no fear. District Officers and Collectors, Junior Magistrates and Engineers all had learned the art of giving orders to natives in a manner that defied disobedience. Sometimes their lives depended on it.

These men demonstrated their superiority in their day-to-day behaviour and in the tone of their voices. They showed, in the way they treated their servants and even in the slightly arrogant style with which they wore their hats, the conviction that the British Empire was all-powerful and benevolent and that those who administered it and policed its boundaries were superior beings who were bringing to the rest of the world the civilized benefits of the British Way of Life.

This lesson was well learned by Chaps and the men of his generation who so often found themselves out on a limb in defence of the Empire and we can not be surprised by how traumatised they were in the 1950s when the whole edifice collapsed. The Edwardian Military Gentleman looked on in horror when the British Way of Life which had been his be-all and end-all vanished along with Imperial pink in atlases of the world. He can be forgiven for feeling that the decline in standards resulted directly from the demise of the Empire and he never completely excused the Church or politicians for failing to provide a moral code to live by once the British Way had been laid to rest.

Speech to graduating cadets; Royal Air Force College Cranwell; December 1957.

"I feel I should say a special word of thanks and indeed welcome to parents and relations for the effort and trouble they have taken to be present today. And I would like, in return, to assure them that these young men are now joining a Service where the hallmark of Cranwell is accepted, respected and welcomed by all. I think, too, I can claim that they are entering a community where they will have a reasonably high standard of ethics to guide them and where they will become valuable members of what we are pleased to call the 'British Way of Life'.

Mid December in Lincolnshire is no occasion for a long open-air speech so I promise to keep you no more than a minute or two longer, but I have one final point. I am convinced that Air Power is the keystone of international politics between the great powers. Until that fact is truly recognized and acted on by all who shape the destiny of this country, I can see little hope of Great Britain regaining the position we used to hold in world affairs.

Biographical Notes. Looking Back From the 1970s. Written in 1971 when in rather a dark mood.

I am now 71. Looking at the world and things in it as they are today the one thought that predominates in my mind is a profound gratitude that I was born in 1899 and not 70 years later. Because I came into this world at the end of the last century I have lived three-quarters of my life in surroundings where the principles outlined in Kipling's 'If', and Polonius' 'Advice to Laertes', the rules in the Sermon on the Mount and devotion through duty to the British Monarch have held some sway in the way people lived their lives and were not mocked from every quarter. I am conceited enough to think that the underlying principles behind these themes have influenced most of my life. Indeed it is from regard for them that I have derived much of the happiness with which I have been blessed. To see these principles challenged, mocked and gradually toppled brings me pain and I am glad that it is only in the sunset of my life that I will have to look on while these things are dishonoured.

It is unrealistic to suggest that for the Edwardian Military Gentleman everything started to go downhill after 1930. For Chaps there are great adventures and achievements still to come: the Second World War and advancing military rank; marriage and a family; honours and awards and the fringes of public life. But for a son of the Empire as they all were in those days things never got much better than they were in 1930, when you could step out of a crashed aeroplane in the rebellious mountains of Afghanistan and declaim to the angry crowd in a language that no one understood, "I am British; take me to your leader." And they would do just that. "Please come to Ali Ahmed Khan and be satisfied."

And Ali Ahmed Khan sent them down the Khyber Road to Jellalabad where they eventually found sanctuary with the remarkable Pir Sahib.

Biographical Notes. Kabul Evacuations.

We were made welcome at the Fort by the Consul and the Pir Sahib's Entourage. The Pir Sahib held a peculiar and immensely influential position in Afghanistan at that time. In a fanatically Islamic country, as a devout and respected religious leader he held great sway over the warring tribes even though they were busy cutting each other's throats.

The Pir Sahib advised us against trying to return to India through the Khyber Pass since there was far too much fighting there and in the intervening countryside for any hope of a safe transit. He had a guest tent pitched for us in an orange grove inside the grounds of his Fort and left us to think over his advice.

The next day I reconnoitred the neighbouring countryside on horseback and found a flattish piece of ground which I reckoned, with the help of some of the Pir Sahib's men could be cleared of major obstacles for use as an emergency airstrip. That night I wrote a letter to Sir Norman Bolton, the Chief Commissioner in Peshawar in which I asked that a Victoria should be sent to my roughly prepared landing strip in one week's time to ferry the two of us back to India. On the Consul's advice I sent this letter by hand of a dependable tribesman who knew secret ways into India. In this letter I particularly asked for a Victoria since it normally landed with its tail slightly up and this combined with its very robust undercarriage would give it the best chance of coping with the imperfections of my rough and ready airstrip. In the same letter I asked that a passing Victoria en route to Kabul might fire off a Very light whilst in the vicinity of Jellalabad to let me know if and when my letter had been received. About 4 days later I saw this welcome acknowledgement from a Vic on its way to evacuate more people from beleaguered Kabul.

During the week following the dispatch of my letter I spent most of my time supervising the work of a posse of the Pir Sahib's men in making this improvised airstrip. We cleared it of major boulders and levelled out some of its undulations. Our work there was made none the easier by some local tribesmen electing to use this particular piece of ground as a battlefield. Despite many interruptions of this kind, by the end of the week I felt confident that our strip was ready to receive a Victoria.

On the appointed day an aeroplane arrived but, in their wisdom, they had sent, not a solidly built and robust Victoria, but an old and relatively fragile Bristol Fighter. The inevitable happened. The hollows, humps and bumps of the improvised landing ground proved too much for the tail skid and rear end of the Bristol. The situation was thus complicated by adding to our ration strength at the Pir Sahib's Fort a third body in the shape of Flying Officer Hancock, the pilot of the Bristol, and we now had on our airstrip one damaged Bristol Fighter which required considerable repair to its tail skid and to several fuselage cross members before it could be flown again.

During the next few days with the help of the Pir Sahib's carpenter, and the leg of a broken chair we got the tail end of the Bristol sufficiently patched up for a safe take-off. At the same time, with more help from the Pir Sahib's men, I was working to improve the state of the airstrip, but, as during the previous week, our work was frequently interrupted by local skirmishes. At the end of a round in this never-ending war, one of the leaders rode over to the place where I had taken cover while the bullets were flying around and invited me to help myself from a huge coffer crammed with gold coins which was strapped to a pack pony. His Indian interpreter said that it would be discourteous of me to refuse since the man wished to make known his friendship for the British. I took out a handful and thanked him. Whereupon he nodded his approval and rode off into the blue. The coins were rouble pieces bearing the Czar's head. Later I had some melted down to make a wedding ring for my wife and two more were fashioned into cuff-links which I still wear.

Letters to his Mother and Fiancée. Written in January 1930. *Dramatis Personae* in the Pir Sahib's Sanctuary.

Last November when the rebellion first broke out the British Consulate was looted by the rebels. The inhabitants were robbed of everything they possessed and the House was burned to the ground simply because it was owned by Amanullah, the deposed King, and on loan to the British for their Consulate. The Consul himself, Khan Sahib Mohammed Jehangir Khan (we called him Shylock) was an old friend of the Pir Sahib and, being suddenly homeless, he betook himself and his Staff (10 in all) to the Pir Sahib's Fort at Charbagh and they were still living there under his protection when we appeared on the scene.

The British Consul was very good to me but as a man I disliked him intensely. He was an Indian Babu of the worst type; oily, self-satisfied, under-brained and slow-thinking. Never before have I held converse with a more conceited fellow. *He could sit down and talk about himself literally for hours on end in the most vainglorious manner without taking a breath or turning a hair. He was a bore to listen to but to look at he was worse. He must have been 6ft 2 or 3 and admitted to 26 stone but I suspected him of more. He didn't walk, he rolled. His greed was appalling and to watch him eat was perfectly revolting. His average consumption of meat was a sheep a day and he had to have his little extras like 2 or 3 pounds of beans or a pound or two of dried grapes or nuts just to help things down. Naturally, being a Mohammedan he used neither fork nor spoon, only nature's implements. Thank Heaven it was not often that I had to see him during his meal times, which, I may say, seemed to last for most of the day.*

Next to 'Shylock' on the consular staff was Mohammed Afzal Khan, an Indian Clerk of the real first-class type who had served his time in the Indian cavalry. He came from a very fine family of fighting Pathans who had served the Government in some way or another for generation after generation. He was a good man and I found his companionship quite stimulating during the last week after Davies had gone. He lent me a copy of Kipling's From Sea to Sea — *a remarkable book to find in the possession of an Indian clerk.*

The other 8 of the consular staff were various servants of little importance except for the cook. He was an Indian from Lahore — an aged and bearded Hindu who said he was 78 years old but was probably more. In his youth he served in Lord Roberts' Mess in Kabul and trekked with him on the famous march to Kandahar. Now, poor chap he was ending his days endeavouring to satiate the boundless appetite of Khan Sahib, the Consul. No sinecure I can assure you. Davies and I were pleased to find this old cook amongst the ménage at the Fort because although he had been with 'Shylock' for 4 years, before that he had been cooking for British Sahibs in India for almost as long as he could remember. He knew what we would like even if he couldn't produce it and he did his best to make the goat and rice and sheep, or whatever our meal was, taste as good as possible. He used ghee to cook with and I missed the taste of butter; there wasn't much lobster mayonnaise either. He made custard every night and it wasn't 'Birds' — the real home-made stuff made out of eggs and milk from the Pir Sahib's farmyard.

...Then there was Buttercup. She was the living counterpart of her namesake in HMS Pinafore. *She was an old Afghan woman, hefty yet haggard who held some influential position in the Pir Sahib's household; exactly what, we never discovered but she had a tongue that wagged incessantly and the men folk were in obvious awe of her. It was amusing to watch her telling off a delinquent among the staff, probably a burly,*

hairy-chested man with a couple of knives in his belt and possibly an Automatic as well. Buttercup took an immense interest in us and I believe she must have had something to do with the Commissariat department because she used to appear at odd intervals with some little delicacy for us secreted in the folds of her voluminous black garment. One day it would be pomegranates, then some sweet-meats or possibly a tray of walnuts and raisins. Whenever she appeared she would put whatever she had brought inside the tent and then stand by the tent flap chattering away in Pushtu, not a word of which could we understand...

We got on very friendly terms with the children. One little Afghan infant aged about 5 attached himself to me permanently and used to wander about with me all day holding tightly to my little finger... each of the children had a catapult of sorts and we rigged up a target and ran a shooting gallery presenting oranges or pomegranates as prizes.

One day one of the Pir Sahib's servants brought me a watch that had stopped. By sheer luck I managed to get it going again for him. After that, each evening they used to come in by twos and threes and I would play around with their watches and poke them about with a pin and a broken knife and I made a few of them better but most of them worse. They appeared equally delighted whatever happened.

That evening, after a meal, we got a message that the Pir Sahib himself would give us audience and we were admitted to the Fort itself. We were led down long, low corridors turning at right angles every now and again until eventually we arrived at the innermost room in the Fort — the kernel as it were — and here we beheld a most impressive sight. We were in a low-ceilinged room lit only by the dim, religious light of a single candle. At one end, on a raised platform sat the Pir Sahib. He was squatting on his haunches after the native fashion and clothed in a resplendent poshten. He looked most patriarchal with his white beard and genial countenance. He was practically white of skin and had a merry twinkle in his eye. He had obviously not lost any of his sense of humour despite his eighty years. Surrounding his 'Throne' squatted some dozen or more of his personal servants watching their master with obvious pride and adoration. Two chairs had been brought in for us and having salaamed the old boy we took our seats and held converse with him. Then if ever I longed to be a linguist! Unfortunately he spoke only two languages, Pushtu and Arabic, so we had to converse using old Shylock as our interpreter. The Pir Sahib was particularly interested in us coming from Baghdad and was very keen to hear all we could tell him about the modern city compared with Baghdad as he knew it in his youth. He also confirmed that the road to India would be too dangerous for us to attempt and encouraged us in our plans for an air evacuation. He was a most extraordinarily broad-minded and generous man. For there he was, a veritable Pillar of the Islamic World happy to extend the shelter of his sanctuary not only to us Christians, but also to several Hindus — mainly merchants who had run into some kind of trouble along the way.

I came away from Afghanistan with a profound respect for the Mohammedan religion. The Afghans are devoutly religious — almost fanatically so — and living amongst them one could get a much greater insight into what their religion really meant to them than was possible when I was simply a Sahib with Mohammedan servants. I think sometimes they are inclined to overdo the ritual, but certainly Islam is a very 'Live' religion and their code of honour is very high indeed.

...you will have guessed that what I missed most of all in the whole show, the greatest tragedy of all, was lack of 'baccy. Luckily I left Risalpur with a full pouch and Davies very generously gave me what he had with him (Perhaps in the hope of getting some respite from the stream of crossword puzzles and arithmetical problems). *And by that means I did not smoke my last pipe-full till the seventh day. After that I gave way to cigarettes. There was a boundless supply of these; the worst and cheapest kind manufactured in Calcutta, but they were a smoke and as Kipling rightly said, "A woman is only a woman, but a good cigar is a smoke..."*

Biographical Notes. Kabul Evacuations.

Davies' knee was by this time in need of proper medical attention so as soon as the emergency repairs were completed on the Bristol Fighter I got Hancock to fly him back to Peshawar. He took with him another letter from me undertaking that if they gave me another week I would have our airstrip suitable for a Bristol to land on and I asked them to send one for me in 7 days' time. The next week I spent in further work on the airstrip by day and in the evenings I read a couple of volumes of Kipling lent to me by the Consul's clerk, pressed on with my amateur watch-making and during a further audience discussed our different religious faiths with the magnificent Pir Sahib.

At last the Bristol came back for me. This time it landed without incident and 40 minutes later I was drinking beer in the Peshawar Club. Then to the pleasant application of razor and toothbrush last used 3 weeks earlier.

The whole Empire celebrated the successful conclusion of the Kabul evacuation. Sir Francis Humphrys and his wife were both honoured by King George V and Flight Lieutenant Ivelaw-Chapman was awarded the Air Force Cross. Perhaps more important was the fact that he had made a name for himself in the Service and, at a time when promotion in the RAF was painfully slow, that was probably the greatest piece of good fortune that befell him.

The Pir Sahib was doyen of the Al-Gailani family of Baghdad and some further information on this whole interlude came to light during a visit to the home of Fatima Al-Gailani who, in 1991 was living as an exile in London. The Pir Sahib was her grandfather and she was also a descendant of King Inayatullah who was Chaps' distinguished passenger on his only successful flight out of Kabul. She had spent some of her childhood in Jellalabad and remembered being told the story of the two British airmen who had been given sanctuary in the Pir Sahib's Fort. The tale had become folklore in the village and she recognized Chaps' descriptions of the *Dramatis Personae*. The British Consul's family were well known to her and they have apparently lost none of their reputation for pomposity and gluttony. The description of 'Buttercup' gave rise to great mirth. She had apparently terrorized the Pir Sahib's household well into the time of living memory. The carpenter, Jacoub Najar, only died in 1986 and was famous throughout his life as the man who repaired the flying machine with the leg of a chair. He apparently also constructed for Chaps and his co-pilot an approximation of a European lavatory known as the 'Thunderbox' which apparently survives to this day. It resides in the remains of the fort where it is pointed out to children and visitors as an example of the strange ways of the English who once ruled the land.

Sadly the gardens and the orange groves have gone, blasted to pieces by the weapons of modern warfare. Gone too is the tradition of hospitality and tolerance that was a feature of the brand of Islam preached by the Pir Sahib and which so impressed the temporary residents of the sanctuary in 1929. Fatima Al-Gailani spoke vehemently and with flashing-eyed contempt of the Communists *and* the Islamic fundamentalists who have been fighting over her homeland for the last thirty years. "The people want *us* back," she said. "If only the West would help *us* to restore the old ways in Afghanistan."

It was difficult not to agree with her.

CHAPTER 7

RUN UP TO THE SECOND WORLD WAR

During the 10 years between 1930 and 1940 Squadron Leader R.Ivelaw-Chapman, DFC, AFC, RAF, followed a fairly conventional career pattern in the pre-Second World War Royal Air Force. He married in 1930; who else but his sweetheart of 10 years, and started a family. There were postings to flying units in positions of command. He attended the RAF Staff College as a student and shortly after as a member of the directing staff. During this time he was forced to come to terms with the RAF pilot's familiar difficulty whereby the heart is in the sky but the posting is to an unprepossessing office in the Air Ministry. Here he has to struggle with a staff job that neither excites nor stimulates a brain intoxicated with the adventure of flight. Chaps' loyalty to his commanders and implacable sense of duty saw him through this trying time but in his 1970 writings we get a suspicion that rebellion was not totally out of the question. He also pulled strings to get into the air on every possible occasion. We read that he gave short shrift to an attempt by Lord Trenchard to lure him out of the RAF into the Metropolitan Police.

Biographical Notes. Service Memories.

In the summer of 1930 Margaret and I were married and after a honeymoon in Cornwall I reported to North Weald in Essex where I joined Number 56 Fighter Squadron. We were equipped with the Siskin, a single-seat fighter. Although I had flown plenty of single-seaters at Martlesham this was the first time that I had actually been on the strength of a unit operating fighting aeroplanes made for one. This brought me in touch with some new techniques in flying that I had not mastered before. In particular I had to learn how to lead and to follow in formation aerobatics. It was a marked contrast to flying the large and lumbering Victoria but I soon mastered the technique and took great pleasure in it. The squadron put on a display at one of the last Hendon Air Pageants.

I was not with 56 for very long. At the beginning of 1932 I was summoned to the RAF Staff College at Andover as a student. On graduation I embarked on 3 years of staff work at the Air Ministry where the only flying to be had was on rather dull types of 'Communications' aircraft.

Then I got back to flying again when I joined No 6 Flying Training Squadron at Netheravon in 1936. This turned out to be my last full time flying job and brought me in touch with yet one more branch of flying that I had not previously tackled, namely instructing. As I commanded the 'Advanced Training Squadron' I was not concerned with ab initio instruction. The students came to me after they had qualified for their wings and my job was to teach them how to use their aircraft as a weapon of war. Our syllabus therefore included such things as Gunnery, Bombing, Photography, Reconnaissance, Formation flying, Night flying and Air Combat. For this purpose I had a hangar full of that delightful Hawker family, the Hart, the Audax and the Fury. I got a tremendous kick out of the job and spent as much time in the air as I could. However, in due course I was called back to the Air Ministry and given the difficult and rather perplexing task of re-writing the existing 'War Manual — Operations.'

In 1934 I was on Intelligence staff work at the Air Ministry and was particularly concerned with the Air Forces of Czecho-Slovakia and Yugoslavia. At that time, once during one's tour, one was allowed to make a formal exchange visit to the actual country concerned. The usual practice was to get to the country in question by ship or train. It struck me that I might find the Czechs and Yugoslavs, from whom, frankly, I was hoping to gather information, considerably more forthcoming if I arrived by air; and this proved to be the case. I needed to land in Germany in order to reach Prague which was to be my first main stop. Diplomatic relations with Germany were of course strained at the time and the Foreign Office would not permit a service aircraft with RAF roundels to land there or in Austria, however 'unarmed' it most obviously was. So then I achieved what I always regard as a minor triumph by persuading the Finance Branch of the Air Ministry to hire for me a Civil Tiger Moth with civilian registration letters and I got myself a civil flying licence.

Early one morning, soon after, I got into this little Moth with a 1:1,000,000 map of Europe in my pocket. There were no other navigation aids and my suitcase was strapped into the front seat. I felt as happy as a Lord to have escaped, even for a few weeks, from my dismal office in the old Adastral House in Kingsway. The Tiger Moth had a small fuel tank and I remember landing at Lympne, Dijon, Zurich and Linz before fetching up in Prague at our previously agreed time. But there was a small snag to all this. I had a visa accrediting me as an RAF Officer only to the countries of Czechoslovakia and Yugoslavia. In all the other countries that I landed in during the trip, France, Germany, Austria, Hungary and Italy, I had to appear as Mr Chapman, (Tourist.) This entailed a lot of changing into and out of uniform in lavatories and

Met. Offices but it was all part of the fun and I always managed to appear in uniform as Squadron Leader Ivelaw-Chapman RAF at any of my pre-arranged appointments.

The Czechs could not have been more hospitable and my arrival by air did a lot to clear away any stuffiness. I was with them for about a week and they took me around a number of their units and also fitted in a very full social programme for me. I recollect visiting their great spa and health centre at Piestany as well as Olomoutz, Prostejov and their fabulous caves in the Tatra mountains. Bidding them good bye in uniform I had to change back into mufti at Bratislava on the Czech border as I was to spend the night in Budapest in Hungary. That was a great treat in itself. The next day I must have changed back into uniform somewhere because I know I duly arrived in Belgrade dressed as a Squadron Leader.

I found the Yugoslavs just as forthcoming and hospitable as the Czechs though unfortunately I had less time with them. I flew on down to Mostar near the Adriatic where they had a fighter station and from there they motored me to see that gem, Dubrovnik. Other details of that visit escape me now save for a marvellous supper taken in a mountain village and served in the open complete with a revolving spit and an open fire where they roasted a whole sheep and the Proprietor announced the meal with a stentorian cry of "Agneau Roti, Agneau Roti." Leaving Mostar I flew on to Zagreb and to Italy (Trieste and Turin.) Thence to Lyons and back home again via Le Touquet to Hendon where Margaret met me and I gave her a flight over London at the tax-payer's expense.

Biographical Notes. Anecdotes. Zurich and the St Anton Pass. Written 1969.

During 1935 I was on intelligence staff duties at the Air Ministry. In May of that year, in the normal course of business, I landed at Zurich Airport late in the evening with the intention of pushing on to Innsbruck that night. I was flying a civilian Tiger Moth with nothing more than a suitcase in the front seat and a million scale map of Europe to navigate by. I had landed at about 6pm with a cloudless sky and felt somewhat thwarted when the airport Met. officials told me pretty bluntly that I had no chance of getting through to Innsbruck that night. I asked why and with a knowing look at my little Tiger Moth they replied, "Low clouds over the Alps."

Having done a fair amount of flying I felt that I knew better and, having filled up with fuel, I took off in the direction of the St Anton Pass. As I approached the foothills of the Pass I realized that maybe there was something to their forecast as more than wisps of cloud were forming in the valleys. Not a bit perturbed I picked up the railway line that goes through to Austria with a road running nearly parallel to it and pressed on, quite

confident that I could get through. Gradually the sky darkened and I found
that the clouds were getting much thicker and the cloud base much lower as
I climbed towards the St Anton. Then, not unnaturally the railway line
disappeared into a tunnel, but even that did not dismay me as I still had the
road to follow. Three minutes later I was forced to concede that the Swiss
forecasters were right for I found myself at tree-top level with the road
climbing above me into thick cloud and with only just enough airspace
between the two sides of the valley to do a tight circle in my little Moth.
There I circled for a while but soon, reminding myself that I was a sane
married man with a small daughter at home, I swallowed my pride, turned
and arrived back at Zurich with my tail between my legs just as the last of
the daylight was disappearing.

They were very kind. They did not say "I told you so," and I was off
again at 4.30 am the next morning to a reward that my arrogance of the
day before scarcely deserved. There was not a cloud in the sky above, only
a few wisps of cotton wool lying in the valleys well below the snow-capped
peaks. Just as I was clearing St Anton Pass the sun came up over the horizon
and tinged the whole scene deep orange. Sitting as I was alone in an open
cockpit at some 10,000 feet almost the whole of the Swiss Alps were in view
and seldom in 40 years of flying have I seen a grander panorama.

On return from the trip to Eastern Europe, Chaps was met at Hendon by
his new wife Margaret. He was deservedly well pleased with himself not
only for the successful completion of a great flying adventure, but also for
his ingenuity in arranging things so that the Air Ministry had to foot the
bill. There was no way of recording the number of hours that the Moth had
flown and it probably was not due to be returned to its owners immediately.
So why not take the lady up for a joy ride over London?

In his haste to get his wife into the air before any one who might
disapprove could notice what was going on Chaps omitted to secure the
harness around her in the open front cockpit. Margaret apparently felt a
little insecure as they cruised around over Hendon and North London. Then
suddenly the nose dropped and the speed built up and the pilot pulled up
into a loop. If a loop is correctly flown the loadings are positive throughout,
even when the aircraft is inverted. In other words centrifugal force holds the
occupants in their seats. If the loop is too slack or if flying speed is lost
while at the top, the G force passes through zero to negative and the fliers
hang in their straps. "What straps?" thought Margaret Ivelaw-Chapman, his
wife of two years and mother of his daughter, as the streets of London
reappeared beneath them.

The editor of this work might never have been conceived if Chaps had
essayed a Slow Roll.

Biographical Notes. Early Days of the 1939-45 War.

After I had been at Netheravon for far too short a time and now with a daughter aged 2 and a son aged 0 I was dragged away from that pleasant job back to the Air Ministry and engaged on the rather urbane task of re-writing what was known as the RAF War Manual: Part One — operations. Dull though this title sounds it was a heavy responsibility as the war clouds were gathering over Germany and we all now knew that War was imminent. We lived for a year at Thames Ditton where I did much of the writing at home and made frequent visits to the Staff College and the Air Ministry to gather all the up-to-date ideas on air warfare.

After about a year and with the War Manual completed I was posted back to the Staff College on the directing staff which was another stimulating assignment. But all of us there could feel the tenseness of the political situation and before I had really played myself in the war came along and I found myself in my pre-determined war appointment on the staff of HQ Bomber Command which was first at Iver in Bucks under Sir Edgar Ludlow-Hewitt and later at High Wycombe under Sir Charles Portal. As a Wing Commander I had rather a dull job in one of the subordinate sections of the Operations Staff. I can't remember many of the details now save one bit of nonsense that it was my task to pass on to our flying units in Bomber Command on behalf of the general staff of the French Air Force. During the period of the 'Phoney War' the French were terrified, quite understandably, of our bombers crossing French territory at night because their presence created a very difficult problem in differentiating between friend and foe. To this end the French Air Staff devised a complicated system called the 'Plan de Balisage'. It was based on the coloured lighted buoy system used for the navigation of tortuous rivers. Every night, using a special code that was only announced in Paris 3 hours before sunset, a system of lighted beacons was put into operation, the layout of which changed with the code. All friendly aircraft flying over French territory were supposed to pick their way beacon to beacon on a zig-zag course over the area concerned. It was all very clever and logical but to an airman, sometimes in cloud, sometimes short of fuel, sometimes not too sure of his position and always in a hurry to get to his destination these compulsory deviations from a pre-planned navigation course became just a 'Bind' and were soon ignored. My sympathy was firmly with the pilots and I had but little stomach for that part of my staff work.

It is interesting to find out how an up-and-coming young Staff Officer spent his free time in 1938 when not engaged in rewriting the RAF Manual of Operations. One of the things that he did was to organize Scavenge Hunts.

14. 'One little Afghan infant aged about 5 attached himself to me permanently and used to wander about with me all day holding tightly to my little finger' (p.77).

15. Hawker Hart, frontline day fighter, 1935.

16. Mrs Ivelaw-Chapman with the children in the garden at Oxshott.

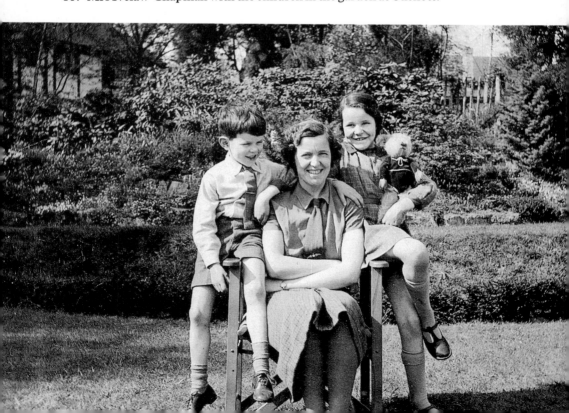

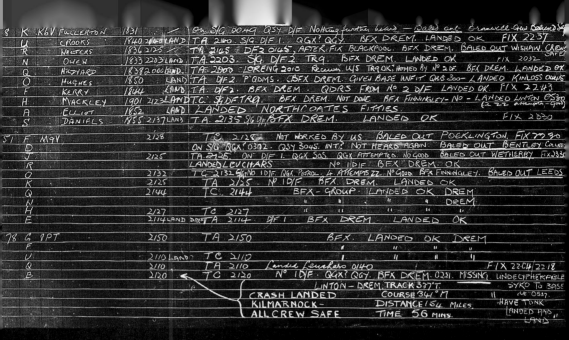

17. Linton Ops Board.

18. Group-Captain Ivelaw-Chapman, Director of Policy, War Office, 1943.

When Churchill ordered: Kill the Air Commodore

WINSTON CHURCHILL ordered the assassination of one of the RAF's most senior officers just a month before D-Day, war historians have only now revealed.

The officer, Air Commodore Ronald Ivelaw-Chapman, had been flying over occupied France, helping to plan the Allied invasion, when he was shot down and captured by the Germans.

He ought never to have been on that flight. He had disobeyed an order that no one with his inside knowledge of the invasion plan should put himself in danger of falling into enemy hands.

So Winston and his war chiefs decreed: "Use every available member of the French Resistance and as many of our men as you need to bring back Air Commodore Ivelaw-Chapman—or eliminate him."

by John Clare

SIR RONALD: He knew too much

19. *News of the World*, 27 May, 1979.

20. An Elsham Wolds Lancaster. The bomb aimer's compartment from which Chaps and Joe Ford observed the raid is visible.

The devious ingenuity of some of the tasks is typical of Chaps, as is the fact that the whole programme was retained and faithfully recorded in a scrap book that never saw the light of day until after his death.

Scrap Book Number 3. June 12th 1938 was a Sunday. It was Chaps' and Margaret's 8th Wedding Anniversary.

WESTON GREEN HOUSE, THAMES DITTON.
JUNE 12TH 1938
SCAVENGE HUNT

'*Notes. First and Foremost this is not a race against time.*

2. The idea is that you work in teams of 3 or 4 in a car and you can push off from here as early as you like after 6pm. You then go round the countryside and collect the various exhibits named on the attached list. When you've got as many of them as you can, in any order you like, bring them back here and the Judge, Dr Harkness, will award them marks on merit.

3. Any questions? Ask R I-C or M I-C.

LIST OF ITEMS

1. A red, a grey, and a platinum blonde hair, but not from any member of the party.

2. A duck's egg autographed by an ELDORADO Ice Cream man.

3. Twenty Cigarette ends in a coconut shell.

4. The address of the SMITH whose telephone number is Willesden 6284 written on a 3d used trolley bus ticket. The telephone must not be used, not even to ring directory enquiries.

5. A completely round stone wrapped in a sheet of today's News of the World.

6. An Oak, An Elm and a Chestnut leaf.

7. A Horseshoe, a Croquet ball, a gas mantle and some genuine confetti.

8. There is this evening a 7.8 pm train from WATERLOO to GUILDFORD which stops at SURBITON, HINCHLEY WOOD, CLAYGATE, OXSHOTT, and COBHAM stations. We would like the number of the leading coach of this train written on the back of a menu card for today of any local pub or hotel.

9. The most original article of any description that you can find.

10. Whilst on tour:

a. One member of the team must do a bit of knitting to the pattern on view in the drawing room. b. One member of the team must learn by heart and on his return recite before the Judge — and the rest of the assembly — the first five verses of the 'Wreck of the Hesperus.'

Lady Ivelaw-Chapman, whose memory for such details is vivid, recalls that The Most Unusual Object prize was won by the team who produced a lavatory seat from a famous London hotel, though highly placed and infinitely more menacing was a child's gas mask brightly coloured and camouflaged as Mickey Mouse.

British military thinking at the start of the Second World War was often stultifyingly conservative. Long serving ex-First World War staff officers of Chaps' age and seniority must take some responsibility for this. It was not that they were incapable of original thought and ideas, it was simply that they didn't consider that it was their duty to declare them. The ludicrous *Plan du Balisage* is an example. In spite of a conviction that the plan could not work, Chaps never apparently considered going to Sir Charles Portal and advising him accordingly. He simply sat in his office at Bomber Command and gave the Plan his best shot. Original thought was not encouraged in fairly junior staff officers, nor was anything that might be taken as criticism of superiors.

Biographical Notes. Service Memories.

After 9 months at High Wycombe I was given the acting rank of Group Captain and sent up to Linton on Ouse near York as Station Commander in No 4 Group Bomber Command ...

CHAPTER 8

LINTON

Biographical Notes. Early Days of the 1939-1945 War.

At Linton there were 2 Squadrons of the ancient twin-engined Whitley bomber, a relatively slow aircraft, even for its time, with no great bomb load capacity but with prodigious endurance. On some occasions a dozen or so of these Whitleys took off from Linton about 2 hours before sunset in the early summer, flogged their weary way across France to Turin which they bombed at night and then toiled back home again, landing well after dawn the next day. The casualties among the aircrew in those Whitleys ran pretty high since they had little speed and not much room for manoeuvre when heavily laden and under anti-aircraft fire. Among the most determined — and to some extent lucky — of the Captains of Aircraft on the Squadron's strength at that time was Leonard Cheshire whose name later became a byword for bravery whilst he was serving and for selflessness after he retired.

I did no operational flying myself but tried to produce an efficient base for these aircrew to operate from. But my efforts were often frustrated by the Germans whose Intruders would dart in across the East Coast and bomb the runways and shoot up everything on and around the airfield.

I was up at Linton during the Battle of Britain but after about 10 months there I was called back on to Staff work again, this time in the Air Ministry in Whitehall. I handed over command of the Station about midday and flew back down to London in my Hart to take up my new post. At 'Briefing' the next morning in the Air Ministry I learnt that my successor, Group Captain Frank Garroway who had survived all the heaviest Blitz during the Battle of Britain in London had been killed on his very first night at Linton on Ouse by a bomb from one of the German Intruders.

"Is that it?" one is tempted to ask. "Is that all that Chaps has to say about one of the most dramatic episodes of the war; the time when Great Britain, standing alone against an army who had conquered most of Europe, launched the first hesitant counter-offensive against Germany?" That indeed is all he had to say. He records no opinions, no feelings, no vivid memories and no conclusions. It is as though he has expunged from his memory everything but the factual details of his life during those nine months and we can only try and make a logical deduction as to why.

In a lot of ways Group Captain Ivelaw-Chapman, DFC, AFC, Station Commander RAF Linton on Ouse in 1940, was caught up in a terrible human tragedy. He was the middle man in a drama that could only end in tears. His superior officers at Group Headquarters and the Air Ministry made all the strategic decisions and issued the orders. Chaps had to implement them. "Tomorrow night 20 Whitleys from Linton will bomb Turin," and Chaps' duty would be to see that the whole complicated process of getting twenty aircraft crewed, armed, fuelled and launched into the hostile sky took place as per directive.

A raid across Europe must have been a nightmare for the aircrew. Chaps' description of the Whitley bomber, however stilted, is quite accurate. He might have added that it carried no navigation aids at all and that it was particularly susceptible to icing; its air to ground communication facility was poor and its bomb sight rudimentary: hardly an encouraging machine in which to run the gauntlet of night fighters and flak, search-lights and natural hazards on a 13-hour jaunt to Turin and back. But for the aircrew there was the gratification of the Nation's thanks, and the uplifting knowledge that they were spearheading the country's retaliation against the tyrant.

"No bombs will fall on German soil," said Goering. "And none on Italian soil," echoed Mussolini. But they did, and in 1940 they fell mostly from Whitleys, to the eternal credit of Leonard Cheshire and his contemporaries flying out of Linton on Ouse and similar stations in 4 Group Bomber Command.

It must have been possible for the aircrew at Linton to set off on their raids over Europe with something of the fatalistic bravado of the Light Brigade; but for the Station Commander who sent them away, night after night, the tension must have been almost unbearable. Chaps was a night bomber man himself and we have heard about his difficulties in navigating around England in a Hyderabad. He was experienced and knew the realities of a Whitley raid to Turin. Without aids, and navigating by Dead Reckoning on inaccurate weather forecasts, the bombers could not be certain of reaching or even locating Italy, let alone their target. If the night was clear and the Italians had left all the lights on, the pilots might see and identify a big town, but the bomb sights were so inaccurate that they simply could not hit specific targets and in any case the bomb load was small with low explosive efficiency. The Group Captain with his Staff training must have known how tragically wasteful these raids were in men's lives, a resource which surely should have been husbanded for the great bombing campaigns to come. And on a more personal level he must have felt for his aircrew the responsibility of a Father. They were his boys and on most evenings as the sky darkened he had to wave 20 Whitleys off on the tarmac and wait in anguish until only half that number struggled back in the small hours of the morning.

And the Station at Linton itself was not secure. The German Intruders found easy pickings there. The runways were bombed as the aircraft took off and on homecoming the tired crews were shot out of the sky even as they lowered the wheels for their final landings. In vain could the Station Commander appeal for fighter cover and airfield defence. Such things were not available in 1940 in Yorkshire because in the south of the country a much more desperate battle was in progress.

The Edwardian Military Gentlemen, as personified in the early years of the Second World War by Group Captain Ivelaw-Chapman at Linton on Ouse, never permitted themselves to question the policy decisions of their superiors. Nor did they consider it honourable to disagree with them in hindsight when the heat of the moment had passed. In some ways this obsessive loyalty is one of the characteristics of this group of men that the present generation finds most difficult to understand. Surely, if a subordinate commander believes passionately that his superiors are mistaken, he should try to the best of his ability to get the questionable policy changed, and when it comes to memoir writing he is entitled to say, "Of course I knew all along that High Command was in error when it laid down such and such policy." That may have been the way in the American armed forces and since the Second World War our senior officers have moved steadily away from hidebound conformity. In the Gulf War it was seriously suggested that the decision to cease hostilities was at least in part due to the individual officer's unwillingness to continue killing an enemy no longer able to defend himself; A laudable step in the advance of civilization, but not the way of the Edwardian Military. To them a war was a war and the quickest way to end it was to win it, and you didn't win wars if Group Captains gave anything less than their whole-hearted and unquestioning support for the policies laid down by their Commanders.

Chaps' description of his time at Linton is terse and devoid of opinion and comment simply because any comment would have been critical of the policy he was forced to carry out. During those nine months, he was overseeing a disaster and he knew it, but we have to look to his anecdotes and his scrapbook to get an inkling of what life was really like in those days.

Anecdote. The Magnificat.

In the second half of 1940 the Germans regularly sent fighter bombers of the Luftwaffe over the North of England to beat up our bomber airfields. The general object was to prevent our aircraft taking off and to harass them on their return. They also used cannon and bombs to knock out control and communication facilities and to create as much mayhem as possible. I was Station Commander at one of our bomber stations, Linton on Ouse just north of York. On one Sunday morning during my tour there I invited the Chaplain in Chief of the RAF, who was in the area, to take a voluntary Service for those of my airmen and aircrew who could get away from their jobs and wanted to attend. Quite naturally the Vicar of the neighbouring village Church hearing that our Chaplain in Chief was in the area asked Canon Jago to preach a sermon in his Church at Evensong. Margaret and I thought that we should help swell the congregation that evening and there was a fairly full Church. Our good intent, however, was thwarted by a German Intruder Bomber who appeared not long after the Service began and who, by the sound of it, was dropping bombs all round the airfield and shooting up anything he could see with cannon fire. Despite the noise outside, the organist bit his lip and played on. The vicar, unruffled, maintained the even tenor of his voice but half way through the Magnificat a large portion of the transept fell in and glass was crumbling from the windows all round the Chancel. This was too much. The organ ceased abruptly; most of the congregation plus the Chaplain in Chief and the vicar took such cover as was afforded by the pews of the ancient Yorkshire village church. It was all over pretty soon but as the dust settled the Clerics and I decided it would be best to call off the rest of the Service. This was the first and I hope the last time that I heard the Magnificat begun but not ended.

A summer's evening and Chaps and Margaret were at the Station. The Whitleys were airborne and in the normal order of things the CO and his wife were helping those left behind get through the agonized hours of waiting before the first of the bombers came home. We two children and our governess were resident in Tollerton Lodge, a grey Victorian building a few miles out of Linton which served as the 'Dispersed Residence' of the Station Commander, Linton on Ouse. At about 10 o'clock the Heinkels struck the airfield.

In a few seconds all was chaos. The lights were out. The control tower received a direct hit and was burnt out. The anti-aircraft defences couldn't see what to shoot at; no one could tell how badly damaged the runway was; and the first Whitleys were due back in an hour or two. Overhead an aircraft could still be heard. Was it one of ours, lost or damaged and waiting to land, or one of theirs with bombs and shells still retained to attack anything that moved on the airfield?

Chaps went about his business as CO, barking orders for fire crews and ambulances and sending out parties to fill the craters, if they could find them, so that there would be a few hundred yards of serviceable runway for the homecoming Whitleys to land on. He was also making decisions; to light an emergency flarepath for his aircraft or to leave the field in darkness and deprive the Intruders of a target; to divert his bombers to a safer airfield or risk everything trying to get them back into Linton. What was the weather forecast? How much fuel did they have left?... and Margaret was naturally desperately concerned for her children. Was Tollerton Lodge intact or had a stray bomb reduced the house and her family with it to rubble? She set off in total darkness to feel her way round the airfield taxiway that would lead her to an exit gate near Tollerton village.

It was fallen telephone wires that brought her grinding, low gear progress to a halt. The strands enveloped the old Rover 12 like a fish trap and gently brought the car to a standstill. She stepped out into the night that smelled of fire and destruction and discovered that the front wheels were teetering on the edge of a 25 foot bomb crater that straddled the taxiway. The fallen wires had prevented the car and driver blundering to almost certain destruction.

All was well at the Lodge. We children and the governess were crouched in the cupboard under the stairs drinking cocoa. "Did you hear the bang Mummy? It was really close."

"Yes, I heard it."

The governess, more aware of what was going on, enquired nervously if it was all over, and was the aircraft, still grinding round overhead, one of ours or one of theirs? "Don't worry," I piped up, aged four and a half, having learned aircraft sound recognition from the cradle, "That's a Whitley Bomber; one of ours. Could I have some more cocoa please?"

Descriptive Note to Photograph. Scrap Book.

On the night of 11th/12th February 1941 when I was OC RAF Station Linton on Ouse our airfield became completely fogbound just before the 21 Whitleys which had taken off at about 1830 hrs were due back to land after bombing their targets in Germany. It was a traumatic night in our Ops room. The nearest clear airfield was Drem, about an hour's flying time away to the North. The photo of the Ops board that night tells a dramatic tale. Of the 21 aircraft that had taken off from Linton, 6 crews baled out, 10 landed at Drem, 1 at Kinloss, 1 at North Coates Fitties, 1 at Leuchars, 1 crash landed and 1 only landed back at Linton after 2 unsuccessful attempts at 0530 hrs after having been in the air for some ten and a half hours.

Letter from Group Captain Lord Cheshire, VC, OM, DSO, DFC. Dated 24th October 1991.

"....at the same time Chaps stands out clearly in my mind as one of the outstanding Station Commanders under whom I served. He represented in our minds the best of the regular Airforce requiring a high standard of professionalism and yet with a very human face to him. The Station was run in such a way as to give the Squadrons the best possible opportunity of working to capacity. He took an intense interest in all of us, even to the point of knowing the junior officers on the squadron by name and actually, I suspect, knowing quite a good deal about us as individuals.

"If you did anything wrong, as I remember I once did, you walked into his office knowing that you were probably going to be 'For it' unless you had a good answer. Mine wasn't very good but he gave me the benefit of the doubt and I can still see the look on his face which seemed to indicate to me: 'You haven't fooled me for a moment, but I'll let you go.'

"Having a Station Commander whom we really respected, whom we knew took a deep personal interest in what we were doing and was always there when the aircraft came back did make a very great difference. Also having some one to look up to as an example of the best in RAF tradition made a great impact on us. Watching him at work prepared me for later days when I was to assume higher command than a mere Flying Officer."

CHAPTER 9

D-DAY

"WHEN CHURCHILL ORDERED KILL THE AIR COMMODORE." This headline appeared, significantly, one year after Chaps died. It stems from the 5 weeks in 1944 when Air Commodore Ivelaw-Chapman was a fugitive in German-occupied France after having been shot down in a Lancaster on a bombing raid. In order to try and establish why the Prime Minister gave this remarkable order we must examine Chaps' duties while posted to the Air Ministry during 1942 and 1943. His journals are unforthcoming. He glosses over this period by suggesting that staff work is of no interest. This is probably because his work was so highly classified that he could not bring himself to commit any facts to paper even 30 years after the event. There are, however, clues in the journals and scrap books, and a study of the Invasion of Normandy allows us to build up a picture of where Air Commodore Ivelaw-Chapman fitted in to the dramatic world of the Cabinet War Room, the Combined Chiefs of Staff and the planning for 'Overlord'. The designations of his postings at the Air Ministry in 1942 and 1943 were Director of Plans and Director of Policy.

The Duties of an Air Commodore staff officer were very different from those of a Wing Commander who simply had to implement plans and policy that were put in front of him. The more senior staff had actually to make the plans and to advise the very senior men who sat on the war cabinet and the Chiefs of Staff committees. The Prime Minister, for example, might say, "The War effort would benefit enormously from the disruption of German tank-making capacity in Bavaria. Let me have your thoughts on that would you, Air Marshal, and as soon as possible." The Air Marshal would then summon his senior staff and set them to work planning the most effective way to attack. 'Intelligence' would outline where in Bavaria the tank-making factories were. 'Operations' would calculate fuel and bomb loads. Enemy defences would be assessed and counter-measures planned. The weather conditions, required and forecast, would be noted and an optimum date for the raid calculated; finally the Staff would decide on the actual units, aircraft and even crews who should take part. The Air Marshal would then present the Prime Minister with a full plan along with an assessment of the probability of success and an estimate of the losses that might be incurred and the decision would be taken as to whether a raid should go ahead.

Winston Churchill often chose to summon individual Staff Officers to his committee meetings so that he could receive directly information about critical factors in operational plans. There is evidence that Chaps attended War Cabinet meetings in some capacity while in the role of Director of Plans, Air Ministry in 1943.

Biographical Notes. Appendix. 'Tribute to Sir Winston Churchill spoken by R I-C at a Memorial Service in St Peter's Church, Over Wallop, 31st January 1965.'

> *Perhaps the Padre asked me to speak because I had the privilege of serving*
> *— albeit in a very junior capacity — under Sir Winston in Whitehall during*
> *part of the war and attending a few cabinet meetings over which he presided.*
> *What more is there to say about this great man that has not already been*
> *spoken or written during the past week? Perhaps to us underlings on his staff*
> *the most impressive side of his gifted character was the 'Punch' and*
> *incisiveness with which he issued his orders, and the enormous range of*
> *subjects, some highly technical, on which he was constantly demanding*
> *detailed information. A master of the written word, his minutes were couched*
> *in the most courtly language, often ending up with some phrase as 'Pray let*
> *this matter be given immediate consideration'. But despite this gracious*
> *approach he never spared his staff and as often as not his minutes were*
> *headed 'Action This Day' even though they might have arrived with us at*
> *ten o'clock at night or later. Much was the midnight oil burnt in getting an*
> *answer on some complicated subject sorted and set out by the time on the*
> *following morning that the 'Old Man' had named.*
> *Many of the more ingenious ideas of the war including PLUTO and the*
> *MULBERRY Harbours were his brain-children and only came to success*
> *through pressure from him. It is typical of his pertinacity at that time that*
> *many of his instructions to us to consider this or that plan ended with the*
> *warning, 'I am not going to be fobbed off by any long catalogue of*
> *difficulties that might occur to the Staff.'*

That little speech, delivered 20 years after the end of the war, is absolutely convincing. There can be no doubt that Chaps was present, maybe actually in the cigar-smoke-filled depths of the Cabinet War rooms, while some of the most vital decisions of the Second World War were taken.

But what was the actual plan that Air Commodore Ivelaw-Chapman was party to that gave rise to the Prime Minister's "Silence him" directive in May, 1944? To answer this we must look at the planning for D-Day that started with Churchill's directive to Mountbatten in late 1941. "I want you to work out the philosophy of invasion, to land and advance against the enemy. You must collect the most brilliant planners in the three services to help you. You must devise and design new landing craft, appurtenances and appliances and train the three services to act together as a single force in combined operation."

Mountbatten in turn set out his aims.

"1. To be certain of obtaining a firm lodgement at the desired place on the enemy coast against all known defences.

2. To break quickly out of the beachheads....

3. At the same time to keep the main enemy forces far from the landing area by deception and prevent them, when they have discovered the deception, from moving reinforcements to the landing area faster than the build-up of the invasion force by bombing road and rail communications over a wide area for several months beforehand."

It is in the third of Mountbatten's directives that security is seen to be absolutely vital. General Sir Frederick-Morgan, Chief of Staff to the Supreme Allied Commander, set the grim scenario. He stated that a successful invasion would only (just) be feasible if not more than 12 reserve mobile divisions should be available to the Germans in France, and that in the Caen Area they should have not more than three of these divisions by D-Day, five by D plus 2 and nine by D plus 8. In other words an invasion's only chance of success lay in keeping the actual landing site secret long enough to prevent a build-up of enemy forces to oppose the landings at a time when the invaders were ill-supplied and at their most vulnerable.

Churchill himself was acutely aware of the disasters that could result if invading forces on a hostile shore met determined opposition that had been concentrated to oppose them. Everything had gone wrong at Gallipoli and, more recently, on the Dieppe raid the Allied forces had been expensively repulsed. In each case it was all too obvious that the enemy were prepared for the attack. A similar repulse of the invasion of Europe would be tantamount to a global defeat for the Allied Forces.

A new security classification higher than 'Top Secret' was introduced to cover any information about the real site of the proposed invasion and critical factors about the dates on which the operation was planned to take place. The code word used was 'Bigot'. All possible steps were taken to minimize the risk of members of the planning staff with 'Bigot' knowledge getting into a position where they might be interrogated by German Intelligence. We read of Colonel Sam Bassett who, in the winter of 1943/44, was put ashore from a dinghy to take samples from the proposed landing beaches in Normandy. Had he been captured the whole plan would have been shelved. Ten officers with 'Bigot' knowledge were lost in the disastrous amphibious landing rehearsal at Slapton Sands. Initially the Supreme Headquarters did not know if these unfortunate men were drowned or in enemy hands. Overlord was put on hold until the last corpse was recovered from the sea and it was confirmed that death had kept the 'Bigot' secrets intact.

While the actual Overlord plan was surrounded with unprecedented security a campaign of disinformation was under way to convince the enemy that the invasion would take place anywhere but in Normandy. The 'I was Monty's Double' story was put into operation to convince them that the target was in the Pas de Calais and a complete diversionary 'Softening Up' process was undertaken in the Boulogne/Calais area. And how well it all worked. For the vital 3 days after the D-Day landings the German Armoured Divisions who could have literally driven the Allies back into the sea were in the wrong place awaiting an invasion that never came.

Of course the whole carefully laid plan could have been compromised beyond repair if an Officer with 'Bigot' information fell into German hands at a critical stage of the build up — say in early May of 1944. On 6 May Air Commodore Ivelaw-Chapman survived a night fighter attack on a Lancaster bomber and landed by parachute in France. On the next day the Prime Minister gave the order for his elimination. It is a reasonable assumption that Chaps had attended meetings in Whitehall, probably chaired by Churchill himself, during which plans for the diversionary attacks and the disinformation process had been made and the true location of the Overlord beaches clarified. Small wonder the Prime Minister was greatly disturbed.

CHAPTER 10

THE RAID

Biographical Notes. Service Memories. Evader and POW 1944 to 1945.

For many months prior to the end of 1943 I had been on planning staff work in the Air Ministry, but it was not altogether to my liking and by the end of that year I was posted up to Lincolnshire as a Base Commander at Elsham Wolds. I had three stations under my command, Elsham, Kirmington and North Killinghome, which were equipped with Lancasters and Stirlings. During the next 6 months I did what I could to appear at briefings, de-briefings, intelligence rooms, dispersals, hangars and workshops at each of my three stations as frequently as possible, as well as coping with the inevitable admin work at my Base HQ. Nevertheless I felt I was not really being much use as a Base Commander and was not likely to be until I had at least one operational sortie (in the current war) to my credit. I had some dual on the Lancaster but I was far too aware of my shortcomings as a pilot to offer myself even as a 'Second Dickey'.

Towards the end of April 1944 with D-Day only some 2 months ahead quite a large proportion of Bomber Command's sorties were directed against ammunition depots and other such targets in occupied France as part of the softening up process necessary before D-Day. The Germans had responded by bringing into France many of their top night fighter squadrons and plastering the country with radar stations. The result was that what had previously been regarded as rather a 'cushy' sortie as compared to Berlin, Stettin or the Ruhr was now beginning to take its toll among our squadron crews. Nevertheless, if my memory serves me right, and I am writing in 1972, a sortie over occupied France only counted as half a sortie towards the crew's total tally of operations. The crews, and I shared their view, thought this a little unfair and it crossed my mind that it might help things if I signed on as extra aircrew on one of these sorties. Accordingly at 0015 on the night of May 6th/7th 1944, with my Group Commander's permission I took off from Elsham Wolds as extra aircrew in a Lancaster (No 783 — ULC) of No 576 Squadron with Flt Lt Shearer of the Royal New Zealand Air Force as Captain of Aircraft. Our target was the German ammunition dump at Aubigne Racan, 25 miles north of Le Mans and not more than 120 miles from the Normandy coast.

Do we take this report at its face value or is Chaps still writing under the influence of 30-year-old security restrictions? Did he really embark on this adventure solely to improve the morale of the men under his command with total disregard for the possibility that he might compromise the whole D-Day plans if he was shot down? Why did the Group Commander give permission for him to go on the raid if, as surely must have been the case, he was aware of the sensitive nature of his Base Commander's previous posting? These questions can probably never be answered beyond doubt, but a fair assessment can be made from the scrap books of letters and from consultations with survivors from those days at Elsham Wolds.

Much has been written about Morale. As applied to Bomber Command aircrew in 1944 it could be defined as the spirit that kept them flying night after night in the face of cruel losses on what must have been one of the most terrifying undertakings that men could embark upon. Consider, for a moment the fear that most people feel when in an aeroplane. Compound it a hundred times by long dark hours of tension and add the certainty that you are going to be met by shot and shell and an opposition that is determined to knock you out of the sky. Remind yourself that you are riding a flying petrol tank that will burn you to death if it is ever ignited and that you are carrying enough high explosive to destroy a small town. If the engines malfunction on take off you will blow up; if the undercarriage fails, you will fry when you try to land, and if you survive tonight you will have to go through it all again tomorrow or the next day and next week and the week after that. Chaps knew that the wartime bomber aircrew were remarkable men. He also was aware of the unmentionable possibility of mutiny; the cancer of rebellion that would grow, as it did in later wars from the first aircraft Captain who decided that enough was enough and diverted his crew's endeavours away from the 'Target for Tonight' into the safer skies of self preservation. Air Commodore Ivelaw-Chapman had a feeling for Morale. He understood its importance and he knew how to foster it. He appears to have been most successful in this matter when he demonstrably took the aircrew's side in any differences they had with the rather soulless Staff at Command Headquarters who selected the targets and made the rules. Had Chaps returned from this raid he would undoubtedly have presented a strong case to Group Headquarters for a more reasonable assessment of a raid over France in a pilot's tally of operations. Though this seems rather a petty quibble now, in 1944 the number of operations still to do in a man's Tour was a matter, literally, of life and death. The men would have warmed to their Commander for this public display of effort on their behalf.

We can conclude that during his 6 months at Elsham, Chaps as Base Commander built up a fine relationship with the aircrew under him. In general terms this was probably the greatest contribution that experienced and charismatic leaders of the First World War generation made to the successful outcome of Hitler's War. When Chaps had to decide whether to fly with one of his squadrons on operations or to remain chair borne in the Base Commander's office, even in spite of the burdensome military secrets that he carried which gave him every excuse for staying behind, he donned his Irving Jacket, pulled on his boots, picked up his parachute and, once again, went to war.

Letter to his Wife. Written 6th May 1944. Datelined Elsham Wolds, Saturday Evening.

We always agreed that if ever I really thought it was necessary I'd go off on one of these bombing shows. Well for one reason or another I think I ought to go off with the boys tonight; actually they have had a bit of a knock lately and I think it might serve to pep them up a bit — so that's why I'm going.

Letter to Margaret Ivelaw-Chapman from Walter Sheen, Station Commander Elsham Wolds when Chaps failed to return from the raid to Aubigne. Datelined Elsham Wolds, 7th May, 1944.

"My Dear Mrs Chaps...
I have locked up 'Chaps" quarters and nothing will be disturbed for a few days. If you want anything particularly would you let me know and I will send it on. The rest will be collected and dispatched by the Committee of Adjustment when I give them the word.

All this appears so matter of fact and quite belies how I feel. Chaps was so kind to me that I feel I have known him for years. No other Base Commander could have been so helpful and understanding that I feel like the small boy who finds a hero to worship. Everyone in the Base simply adored him and admired him and they all look so stunned this morning that I feel they are silently voicing their sympathy also...
Yours very sincerely,
Walter Sheen."

Written interview with Joe Ford, one time Flight Sergeant Wireless Operator/Bomb Aimer and member of the crew of Lancaster 783 — ULC on the night of May 6th/7th 1944. Datelined Tatura, Victoria, South Australia 23 July, 1990.

"Q. What did the aircrew at Elsham actually think of Chaps as Base Commander?

A. I recall him at briefing. He always impressed the crews with his brief but telling words. He was obviously concerned by the sheer magnitude of the enemy defences that we had to penetrate to reach the target.

Q. Do you think that morale was actually improved by the knowledge that the Base Commander undertook a raid over enemy territory albeit in the role of passenger?

A. I believe that was so. When our aircraft pulled out of dispersal on the night of the 6th May there were quite a number of bods waving; something we had not seen before. When I returned to the squadron the few people I contacted were proud of Chaps' decision. When I thanked the girl who packed my parachute she was most complimentary about the courage that he had shown."

There is another aspect of Chaps' character that made it almost inevitable that he took part in a raid during the Second World War. We have learnt that he was a compulsive adventurer; clearly he simply could not pass up an opportunity to take part in one of the twentieth century's great experiences. Even if his Group Commander had been better briefed on the security aspect and withheld permission for Chaps to fly with 576 Squadron, somehow the order would have been mislaid or delayed long enough for him to slip away on Ops, just one more time.

Biographical Notes. Service Memories.

There were about fifty Lancs in the stream for the target that night. Flt Lt Shearer took us out there with no untoward event at some 18-20,000 feet in a three-quarters moon with no cloud cover. As we neared the target I crouched alongside Sgt Ford of the Royal Australian Air Force in the bomb aimer's cubby hole as a 'Ring Side' spectator. On the appointed dot second, the marker flares went down from a Pathfinder Mosquito. I was amazed at the accuracy and skill with which these marker chaps had found this depot which later I discovered to be in a nondescript wood with no prominent or lead-in features and stuck well out into the countryside. How they did it astounded me then and still does.

Half a dozen of the stream may have bombed before us and by the time we were running in to the target it was well alight and the conflagration with its periodic vast explosions was a sight I shall never forget. Even Sgt Ford with his long tally of Ops behind him had never seen anything like it before. By the time we left the target it was not so much a 'Brocks' benefit as a burning fiery furnace.

We had settled down on the first leg of our homeward run when our rear gunner suddenly opened up and shouted down the intercom, "Corkscrew Skipper," which Shearer immediately did.

Within seconds there was a flash from a night fighter flare and cannon shot riddled our Lanc all down its fuselage followed by the terrible smell of fire. We had been picked up by radar and a Messerschmidt 110 had been vectored on to us. Then came the first sign of flames in the middle of the fuselage and almost immediately our Captain's order to Bale Out.

Sgt Ford snatched his 'Brolly' and was away. Mine was strapped to the side of the fuselage just below the second pilot's seat. I remember grabbing it and making for the bomb aimer's exit, but at that moment an explosion occurred in one of the petrol tanks and I found myself in the air suspended by a parachute to which, in my panic, I had attached myself by one buckle instead of the more orthodox two. By moonlight from 15,000 feet or so I could see the flat countryside of Normandy below me with the Foret de Perseigne well defined. Our poor ill-fated Lanc, with all its crew save Sgt Ford and myself, had become a ball of fire and I saw the wreckage hit the earth at least a minute before the trees on the edge of the forest loomed up alarmingly close below me and I landed with a bump, badly shaken but otherwise all in one piece. Many months later I discovered that of the 50 aircraft on Ops that night from 1 Group, ours was the only casualty.

For the next 10 minutes, mindful of the briefing I had been given at Elsham some 6 hours earlier, I dug like a beaver and buried my parachute as best I could and made for such cover as the locality offered. It obviously wasn't wise to move far that night because in the three-quarter moon my parachute descent must have been seen by many a German for miles around and the area was bound to be cordoned off. So, having filled my waterbottle from a stream, I curled up in some undergrowth and tried to rest. Not long afterwards I heard the trackers with their dogs passing within a few yards of me, but obviously the dogs had not yet got my scent.

After a restless day trying to place myself on my map, schooling myself to lie still, occasionally peering at the landscape through peepholes in the undergrowth and turning over in my mind a dozen different plans for my first night's march I finally decided to head south when the sun went down; heading for the Brittany coast with the Pyrenees as a long term alternative.

Progress was slow because the moon lit up the fields and I had to walk bent double along the hedgerows. As an example of the state of mind I was in, I was moving, as I thought pretty stealthily through a partially wooded area when I spotted ahead by some 20 yards a German Sentry with his back to me. I guessed I had strayed, by bad luck, upon a German camp of some sort and I stood motionless for a minute or more with my hair standing literally on end. The sentry fortunately had not seen me and without turning round I stepped backwards one step at a time and as noiselessly as *possible in the direction of a tree that I had just passed. When I felt the tree on my back I worked my way round it until it hid me from the sentry and there I remained for about ten minutes. Then gradually I realized that the whole thing had been a figment of my imagination and soon I was walking on again quite happily past the very spot where I had been so certain that a sentry was standing.*

So it went on for a couple of days until one morning I awoke in the middle of a cluster of brambles where I had taken refuge the night before when the moon got too high for further progress. I could see a farm house in the distance and I was gaining a bit more confidence by then and I thought I had a clear enough view of any movement in the area to give way to the temptation to have a wash and shave in a little brook that flowed some 10 yards from my hide-out. Whilst in the middle of my ablutions, from a direction that I had overlooked, there approached an oldish French peasant who was obviously as much surprised to see me as I him. There was no turning back now. If I was to make contact with the French, now had to be the time. We were briefed before take-off on the type of French person most likely to be sympathetic to the allies and this man fitted the description pretty well... and my emergency rations had gone and I was starving.

In my halting French I told him my story which he accepted at once, since even at that distance he had seen our Lanc come down in flames and had heard that at least two of us had survived and had not yet been found by the Germans. He leapt over the brook, followed me into my hideout and we had a friendly chat about this and that; about the war in general and the Germans in particular. I found him particularly sympathetic when he discovered that, like him, I had fought against the Germans in the First World War. Bidding me a temporary farewell he adjured me not to move during the day but he would see what could be done in the evening if his Monsieur le Patron was favourably impressed. Sure enough, by nightfall he was back and led me to a disused farm hut where he told me to stay until he came back at midnight. At around about midnight a much younger and more educated French farmer suddenly and noiselessly appeared at this hut, rushed up to me, threw open my flying overalls and turned his torch on my uniform. Later I learnt the reason for this somewhat abrupt introduction. Sheltering an allied airman in occupied France at that time meant certain death. Despite this it was pretty common especially in the rural districts and the Germans had put out a number of stooges who represented themselves as escaping airmen in order to track down gallant members of the French Resistance. However, the sight of my uniform plus what his farmhand must have told him of our conversation that morning seemed to reassure him and later that night the three of us threaded our way in Indian file in the shadow of the hedges to the farmhouse of Monsieur le Patron.

Le Patron's wife was a very understanding woman. She had guessed that it was food that I needed most, and she had sent with her husband several lumps of sugar for me to get into my system before she put any solid food in front of me. Later that night, by candlelight, I was given a terrific spread in the kitchen of this lowly farmer's house on the outskirts of St Rémy du Plain near Alençon, before being offered the welcome shelter of an attic under the rafters of their thatched roof. That was my home for the next ten days or more. The next morning these kindly and very brave folk brought me a suit of civilian clothes and my uniform, overalls, markings off my underclothes, in fact anything that I possessed or wore that might have identified me as British were duly buried in the garden of a nearby château.

Within the next couple of days another young and intelligent Frenchman arrived in the attic and started quizzing me very astutely about conditions in England. What did a week's ration of butter weigh? How many points went to a quarter pound of chocolates? What film was showing at the Odeon Leicester Square? Apparently I passed my examination, because at the end of his third visit his manner, which up till then had been rather brusque and officious, suddenly changed and he said, "All Right, Air Commodore Chapman, I have let London know that you are alive and with us, and I have got your bomb aimer, Sgt Ford living with a village priest about ten miles from here. I will arrange for you to join up in about a week's time. Maybe I was a bit suspicious at first, but I had to do a bit of checking up with London about you as we don't often get Air Commodores around here."

The date was Friday 12 May, 1944, when Chaps' identity was confirmed by the French Resistance in London. A lot had been happening since he went missing on the night of 6/7 May.

News of the World: May 27, 1979.

"WHEN CHURCHILL ORDERED KILL THE AIR COMMODORE

"On May 8th 1944, almost exactly a month before D-Day Colonel Langley received a phone call from Desmond Morton, the Prime Minister's personal secretary giving the following order;

'Use every available member of the French Resistance and as many of our men as you need to bring back Air Commodore Ivelaw-Chapman – or eliminate him.'

'Is that an Order?' asked the Colonel. Morton confirmed it. The planning of the operation was then handed over to the late Airey Neave, the MP who was assassinated by the IRA in 1979."

So we can assume that the intelligent young Frenchman who examined Chaps' credentials in the attic room in France was doing more than simply protecting the Resistance operatives from German infiltration. He was acting on behalf of the British Prime Minister who was desperate for reassurance that his D-Day secrets were still safe. And by 12 May London knew that for the moment Air Commodore Ivelaw-Chapman was holed up in a safe house. The D-Day plans, however, were only safe as long as the French Resistance cell that was protecting Chaps was itself secure. If it was penetrated and the Air Commodore captured the whole secret build-up to the Normandy landings could only be expected to remain intact for as long as Chaps could resist interrogation.

It is interesting to speculate as to whether Churchill advised Eisenhower that the whole plan might be compromised at any moment during the three weeks prior to D-Day. Such a breach of security would be internationally so embarrassing that the facts were probably not passed on to the Supreme Allied Commander. The Prime Minister, we must assume, kept the whole thing to himself, trusting in Airey Neave to pull his man out of France or a French resistance guard to silence Chaps for ever if capture was imminent. He no doubt also assumed that a man of Chaps' background and sense of duty would not give way easily under interrogation.

By 12 May the Prime Minister and a few of his close advisers knew that Chaps had survived the crash and was being looked after by friends. No one else did.

Extracts from letters received by Margaret Ivelaw-Chapman. Second half of May 1944.

From a Squadron Commander at Elsham Wolds:

"Dear Mrs Ivelaw-Chapman,
    Please accept the sincere sympathies of myself and my squadron for the anxiety you must be feeling for the Air Commodore's safety.
    The failure of his aircraft to return from Aubigne gave every one here a great shock and I know we'll never get another Base Commander like him. Flt Lt Shearer, the pilot, was one of our brightest boys and had got himself out of several tight corners previously. I just can't think what can have happened to them.
    If you would like to write to the next of kin of the crew..."

From Keith Murray; the CO of Number 10 Squadron in the First World War. Last heard of making a dive for safety from his horse on Menin airfield as Chaps indulged in a series of wild stunts and beat-ups on hearing of his posting back to England. Now Chief designer for Wedgwoods and a long-standing family friend, Keith Murray was Godfather to Chaps' and Margaret's son John.

"My Poor Margaret

I am so sorry. Naturally I did not know or I'd have written before this. Please let me know if you hear anything. My chief feeling is one of fury at such a thing happening at all. Why? I've spent a large part of my time wishing that there was a little less bravery about in this war and a little more brains. But alas, don't I sympathize with him! My chief bond with Chaps was a mutual feeling for the 'Flying Boys' and he was essentially one of them. After a tour in the Pest House (The Air Ministry), — however distinguished — as his was, he must have been mad keen to get back flying again. One can't blame him for wanting with all his heart to join the lads at the job.

Was any one seen to bale out? If he got down all right we can certainly rely on him to end up before long in Switzerland or Spain but with the chaos that may come with the coming invasion (?) it may well be months before you hear anything.

So don't lose heart. You are a Service Woman and you know the risks; much better than I do. But I certainly will take it for granted until I hear to the contrary, that Chaps is now, at this moment, steadily working his way towards one of the sheltering neutral borders, and doing a lot of Staff research work on the way.

Take care of yourself
Yours
Keith."

From Bill Dry at the Air Ministry. He was bound by security but was he trying to let her know some good news?

12th May 1944

"Betty My Dear,

Gwen and I are so sorry to hear about all this. But I shouldn't worry unduly. France isn't like Germany and on the quiet we get a good number of folk back from there. The old lad may be sculling about France somewhere (Same like Basil Embry) and he'll turn up......

As Ever, Bill Dry."

From 'Dolly' Gray; he of the bottle of Beaune and the Staff College exam in Baghdad.

"My Dear Betty,

I do hope you soon get some real good news of Chaps. In the mean time I don't like the idea that you may be feeling short of cash; it's so awkward. So I am enclosing a cheque to carry you on till Chaps gets back. Don't hesitate to cash it and spend the money; that's what money's for!

Hope you have not had any 'Doodlebugs' around you. Sir Ralph (Sorley) visited me yesterday — no change.

All the best,
Dolly Gray."

From the Air Ministry, Casualty Branch. Dated 20th May 1944

"Madam,

I am commanded by the Air Council to express to you their great regret on learning that your husband, Air Commodore Ronald Ivelaw-Chapman, CBE, DFC, AFC, Royal Air Force is missing as a result of Air Operations on the night of 6th/7th May, 1944 when a Lancaster aircraft in which he was flying as second pilot set out to bomb a target in enemy territory, and was not heard from again.

This does not mean that he is killed or wounded and if he is a prisoner of war he should be able to communicate with you in due course. Meanwhile enquiries are being made through the International Red Cross Committee and as soon as any definite news is received you will at once be informed.

If any information regarding your husband is received from any source you are requested to be kind enough to communicate it immediately to the Air Ministry.

The Air Council desire me to convey to you their sympathy in your present anxiety.

I am, Madam,
Your Obedient Servant,"

From 12 May, Winston Churchill and a few close advisors knew of Air Commodore Ivelaw-Chapman's whereabouts and situation. Chaps was unaware that the French Resistance were under instructions that he should not be allowed to fall into enemy hands alive. Everyone knew that the invasion was imminent but an exact date had not been set and only a few people knew the proposed landing sites. Spying and counter-spying were at a frenetic level. Mrs Ivelaw-Chapman knew nothing of her husband's whereabouts and was sustained only by hope that he was alive.

CHAPTER 11

EVADER

Biographical Notes. Evasion Journal.

Jacques was true to his word and within 10 days I had bidden farewell to my hosts and was on my way by charcoal-burning truck to the village of Renée about 8 miles away, where I found Joe Ford already ensconced in the attic of another very brave family.

We spent another 10 days there because Jacques had decided, very wisely, that we should not move further southwards until we had established our identity as Frenchmen with the appropriate papers including permits to travel and all that. We both had with us the usual photograph of ourselves in civilian clothes which all aircrew carried with them for this very purpose. Jacques knew all about this and took our passport-looking photos off with him to Paris. In a few days he was back with a complete set of forged papers which turned me into Monsieur Robert Touchard who was an engineer by trade hailing from Albi, a town near the Pyrenees. He had German authority to 'Circulate' in certain areas of France and, not surprisingly, had the same complexion and vital statistics as myself. Joe Ford was similarly equipped though he supposedly came from another town also in the southern part of France.

It was whilst staying at Renée that I made a night visit to a doctor. On landing after baling out one expects to collect a few bruises and I was no exception. Most of these had now cleared up but my left shoulder seemed to be getting more rather than less painful. My host's mother, a very kindly soul, produced a bottle of 'Ellimans' and one evening Joe Ford who had been trainer for a football team in Australia, gave my shoulder a drastic dose of massage. That night I had no sleep at all and the next morning, after a bit of a conference it was decided to take me to see a French doctor some five miles away. Le Médécin had been told who I was but was nevertheless prepared to see me provided I came by night and was examined by candle light. My French Resistance host at this time was a repairer of tractors and other farm implements and had permission to keep a charcoal-burning truck to circulate amongst the neighbouring farms — but by daylight only. Despite this we set off about midnight and with no vehicle lights at all. The first thing that happened was that the engine stalled in the middle of the village on a steep incline and there was no ordinary commotion before we got going again. When we eventually arrived at the doctor's he took one look at my shoulder and pronounced it 'Déboité' (Dislocated) and asked when I had done it. I then realized for the first time that having baled out on one strap instead of 2 I had pulled my arm out of its shoulder socket a fortnight previously. I asked him to put it back in. He merely smiled and said that the time lapse was far too great for that. It was now a surgeon's job and there was nothing further that he could do.

There were four generations of the same family living in the house at Renée where we stayed; Great Grandmother of some 85 years down to young Jean-Pierre who was 6 at that time. Only the two middle generations knew that Ford and I were being hidden in their attic since in occupied France the fewer people that knew of the existence of wandering airmen the better. The only time we left the attic was after Jean-Pierre and his Great Grandmother were asleep when we occasionally got a little night exercise in the closed precincts of the tractor yard. About the second day of my stay there I noticed a piece or two of 'Meccano' lying about in the attic. Bit by bit I found more, and, to while away the time, I started making models with them. My host's mother noticed this and gradually passed up the stairs more and more of Jean-Pierre's toys which had been bought for him in Paris before the war and which were to have been dished out to him on succeeding birthdays as he got older. The long days seemed to pass quicker when I set myself the task of making a model of the Forth Bridge. After we left Renée and moved southwards Jean-Pierre was shown this model but was told that on no account was he to dismantle it. A few months after the war my wife and my family and I, all went back to visit this brave family of Patards at Renée. Great Grandmother had passed away but Jean-Pierre knew all about me and we enjoyed ourselves dismantling the Forth Bridge and talking about the war.

After 10 days with the Patards, Joe Ford and I emerged one afternoon as French citizens complete with French papers and mounted on borrowed bicycles. After the restricted life of the previous three weeks we felt as free as air and we whistled as we rode to a nearby village where we had been bidden to call at a local baker's shop and remark casually that we 'Cherché-d' Gilberte. This we duly did and were promptly taken into a back parlour where we met one of the bravest Frenchwomen it has ever been my privilege to know. She was in her early twenties at the time; born in Brittany but resident in Paris. She was cheerful, with a charming smile and seemed quite unperturbed by her first mission of this sort. She had taken it on without question although the Gestapo were hot on her trail following three years of active and unrelenting work for the Resistance movement. She had come down by train from Paris to shepherd us to the house of a man who lived on the banks of the Loire in Touraine. Undaunted by the prospect, Gilberte actually appeared thrilled at the idea of escorting a very Saxon-looking Australian wearing one shoe and one carpet slipper and without a single word of French, and me in an ill-fitting suit of clothes, with my arm in a sling, not terribly fit and looking, as I thought, every inch an escaping allied airman!

The two-day journey to the Touraine, partly by train, partly by bicycle and an awful long way on foot, had its odd moments. At one interchange station the Paris Bordeaux train arrived so full that there was no seat to be had and Gilberte, with an admirable flow of invective, bullied the Station master into having an extra coach put on in which we travelled first class — with second class tickets — while German soldiers and sailors returning from leave were forced to stand in the corridor. We shared a table at one railway restaurant with two German Corporals, much to my apprehension and Gilberte's delight. My morale was soon restored when Monsieur Touchard (Moi) was required to produce his identity papers to cross a bridge over the River Loire and the German sentry accepted them without question.

At one point there was an air raid alarm and our train was halted at a wayside country station. We, rather stupidly, were travelling in the front compartment next to the engine. I ought to have known better because I knew full well that our fighter pilots were strictly briefed that their attacks on trains were to be directed against the locomotive only; but we have all heard of near misses. There were 12 Mustangs of Fighter Command who had spotted the train and each made 4 or 5 dives at the engine firing their cannon. Together with some French civilians we took cover under the seats and managed to survive. While the wrecked engine was being towed away and another found from somewhere to take us on I noticed in a garden that had been in the line of fire a washing line of nappies. They were clean and dry but peppered with shot holes like targets on a range.

On the same journey, about an hour out from Le Mans, I heard some French civilians in the compartment getting very excited as we passed close to the defunct German ammunition dump at Aubigne Racan. I gathered from their conversation that the depot had been completely gutted, that there had been no civilian casualties and that they were at a loss to know how this depot had been found and so effectively destroyed — and all by night. Naturally I refrained from joining in the conversation!

Soon Joe Ford and I were patiently waiting at our next house for a message from the BBC to say that our sojourn in France was nearing its end. Our new host, Monsieur Lecomte, was a staunch French Resister who from time to time controlled with a hand torch the landing end of

S.O.E. operations. They knew in Whitehall by then exactly where we were and it was planned to send a Lysander to a field not far from M. Lecomte's house. It was to land on an agreed night under the control of my host and having picked up Ford and myself and a French Resister for whom things had got too hot in France, it was to take us back to Tempsford. The timing of all this was to be made known to us by a special code-phrase broadcast by the BBC amongst a whole rigmarole of seeming gibberish. At last one morning, after a fortnight with the Lecomtes, our code word came through on the radio and I was lying on my bed imagining the sound of an approaching Lysander in the early hours of the next morning. We would be bundled into the rear seats; catch a glimpse of the coast of England and step out once again on home soil. I would see my family again and, even more pressing, I could get into Halton Hospital and have a surgeon look at my dislocated shoulder and left arm which now hung painful and immobile by my side.

It was during the night of 7/8 June 1944 that Chaps lay on his bunk in an outhouse of Mr Lecomte's farm at Brain-sur-Allonnes imagining rather prematurely that his return to England was imminent. We should remind ourselves what was going on elsewhere.

Allied Forces had landed in Normandy on the previous day and were desperately consolidating their beachheads. The German High Command knew of the landings but were as yet unsure that this was the 'Real' invasion. The French Resistance were aware that the allied invasion of Europe was under way and that landings around Arromanches were no diversionary attack. They were under instructions to disrupt in any way possible the movement of German armour to oppose the breakout. This information was passed to them largely by the coded messages from the BBC that Chaps mentions hearing as he listened for his own 'Lysander' alert.

Airey Neave of MI9 knew exactly where Chaps was and that his information was still secure. He probably received a daily report from the Resistance cell looking after Chaps which was passed on to the Prime Minister. This we must assume was the condition for allowing Chaps to survive. Churchill's instructions were "Extricate or Eliminate". The MI9 operatives had also delayed the Tempsford operation for nearly two weeks and this we must assume was because they realized that the actual Lysander landing was the critical part of the operation and the moment Chaps was most likely to fall into enemy hands. They therefore waited until 24 hours after the invasion because with every hour that passed the information that Chaps had in his head became less and less potentially damaging.

It is unlikely that Chaps himself knew that the landings had actually taken place and he makes no mention of it in his journal. He was also unaware that he was being watched by his own side and that in the event of imminent capture by the Germans there was probably a bullet waiting to silence him for ever.

After 3 weeks of agonized suspense his wife and close relatives at home knew that he was alive.

Letter from the Air Ministry (Casualty Branch) dated 1st June, 1944.

"Madam,
I am directed to refer to a letter from this Department dated the 20th May, 1944 and to advise you that information has been received that your husband, Air Commodore Ronald Ivelaw-Chapman, CBE, DFC, AFC, PSA, Royal Air Force baled out over occupied territory and is alive and well.

In the interests of your husband and his benefactors you are asked to keep this good news to yourself and not to ask for further information or attempt to communicate with him in any way. It should be appreciated that if your husband is caught it not only means that he will become a prisoner of war but that those harbouring him will no doubt serve the death penalty. In these circumstances it is felt sure that you will co-operate.

His Father is being informed.

Any more definite news will be passed to you immediately it is received.

I am, Madam,
Your obedient servant,"

Letter to Margaret from Chaps' sister Shirley.

"My Dear,
You have never been out of my thoughts these last three weeks, but what happened took away all power of expression in words between those of us who loved him so dearly. I know you will understand why I did not add another letter to the many you will have received. Your marvellous faith and bravery bore us up. Eileen and Mother and I could hardly speak of him to one another — just doing things, doing things to make time pass. Mother's spirit is something to be marvelled at. It seems always to be there, to transcend anything that life can do to her. And now, my dear, I send to you and the children my love and all hope for those happy days to come when we may be able to see him again. God has indeed been good to us. Nancy has been so sweet and

Robin too. They made me feel proud because I felt their sympathy was not just for me because I was desperately unhappy and anxious but that they were grieving too, terribly, for Ron whom they look up to as a man amongst men.

Today we are going to Windybrake to have a large happy tea party. We are of course still smothered, as it were, with speculations about his whereabouts and what will happen to him, but we can only be patient now and wait. By the time you get this letter I think you may know more.

All my love and thoughts to you my Dear,
Shirley"

Biographical Notes. Service Memories. 'Evader' and POW 1944-1945.

My reverie was interrupted by a hoarse whisper of "Gestapo" and I leapt from my bed to find the house surrounded by a bunch of Germans and indeed French collaborators, all heavily armed. My host made a bolt for it but was shot down, not mortally, in his own cornfield and I was soon being driven to Gestapo headquarters in Tours, under escort and handcuffed.

That night was the grimmest I have ever spent. I had rid myself of any British identity. I was in civilian clothes and under the close scrutiny of the Gestapo the forgery of my French papers soon became apparent. I had read about 'Third Degree' methods several times but scarcely believed it. That night I got it to the full; threats, arc lights right up to my face, bullying, a human skull on the table, the parade of the firing squad, physical flogging, and all the rest. After 8 hours on end of this kind of interrogation and at about 3am I was put into a dungeon 3 floors below street level in the old civil gaol at Tours. When the guard had shone his torch into the cell before locking me in I noticed in one corner 3 or 4 boards raised from the floor by a few bricks. There, I thought, I must do my best to get some sleep; but sleep would not come my way because my hands were manacled behind my back and that was just the most painful position for my dislocated shoulder. Earlier that night I had been making up a cock and bull story for the benefit of my Gestapo hosts about how I came to be in that area, and I knew that I would want all my wits about me for the next morning's dose of interrogation. To do this I needed somehow to get some sleep. I then discovered that they had put the hand-cuff on my left wrist higher up my arm than the strap of my wristwatch. With some difficulty I managed to get the watch off and on to the floor. I then got my left manacle down over my wrist bone and thus a fraction of an inch nearer my hand. This just allowed me to get the loop of my manacled hands around my backside and then to step through the loop with my feet, thus bringing my arms round on to my stomach. The diminished pain was an enormous relief and I lay down on the boards and put in about 4 hours' sleep before the key in the door awakened me. My Gestapo guards were not amused when they got me out into the daylight. They accused me of having a key to the hand-cuffs and altogether were very rough with me when they discovered that I had done a bit of a 'Houdini' on them.

The next day, to my bitter sorrow and dismay, I caught a glimpse of Gilberte also manacled and in the same gaol and my spirits dropped to zero. But eventually her luck held and, although she went through a truly appalling time with the same lot of Gestapo thugs who handled me, some 3 months later she escaped from their clutches during another air raid upon a train in which she was being taken to the notorious women's concentration camp at Ravensbruck. She and I met up immediately after the war ended and now she, her husband and her son are among my family's dearest and most cherished friends.

Mercifully for me, after an unpleasant further bout of interrogation, I was eventually able to convince the Gestapo that I was an RAF Officer and I was passed on to the SS who were the uniformed police. A short stay with them and then on to Chartres where I was handed over to the Luftwaffe as a normal Prisoner of War. There followed some relatively mild days of solitary confinement; then 2 operations on my shoulder in a German Hospital; 10 months in a Dulag Luft just outside Frankfurt and then, as the allied forces were nearing, a transfer to Nuremburg where, eventually on my wife's birthday in April 1945, I was liberated by American forces.

Methods of military interrogation have changed since the Second World War. So have the requirements for British fighting men who have been captured. It is now generally accepted that a captive can not be expected to resist interrogation for more than 24 hours. After that any information must be assumed to be compromised. A man in enemy hands is no longer subject to Court Martial if he reveals more than his number rank and name. He is simply expected to delay as much as is physically possible the divulgence of information that will compromise the activities of friendly forces.

Chaps seems to have instinctively followed, under the most intense pressure, the correct counter-interrogation procedures. He out-thought his inquisitors and realized very early on that they didn't know what he knew. When his situation became unbearable he released information of little importance, to buy time, and invented a story that it was impossible to refute.

We must remember that throughout his interrogation he was in agony from his damaged shoulder and at times deprived of light, heat and fresh air 3 floors below ground in a municipal gaol in a foreign town. Can any one, reading of his tribulations not imagine the temptation to shout, "Stop. Get me some pain killers and a doctor for my arm and I'll tell you something about the invasion that could win you the war?" No one in the 1990s would have blamed him, and yet no one who knew the Edwardian Military Gentleman would concede that such a capitulation was ever even feasible. We should salute him. We also should salute Gilberte, who must have been aware that her charge was considerably more important to the British Government than a straightforward evading airman. Had she let slip a whisper of this to her torturers, Chaps might have had to face an even more intensive interrogation which he might not have survived.

News of the World Article. May 27th 1979.

"Professor Foot added: 'I am sure that Ivelaw-Chapman was never told that he came very close to being shot by his own men. Airey Neave would never have told him — he was not that kind of man. But Ivelaw-Chapman was brought up in the old school tradition. He knew that the information that he had could never be allowed to fall into German hands. I am sure he would have died for his companions if necessary.' "

MI9 Debriefing Form completed by R I-C on repatriation in 1945. Classified SECRET.

On 8 JUN the Gestapo raided the farm where F/Sgt Ford and I were staying at BRAIN-SUR-ALLONNES. I was captured. F/SGT Ford was in another farm building at the time and was not captured with me. During the raid our host, the Frenchman who owned the farm, was wounded and captured. He was taken with me in the car and admitted into a civilian hospital in SAUMUR. On the same day I was taken from SAUMUR to the Gestapo HQ at CHAMBRAY. My hands were manacled behind my back from the time of my capture. I was interrogated as a suspected Secret Service Agent but for some time I refused to give more than my number, rank and name. I was slapped in the face, beaten on the shoulders and buttocks with a rubber whip, and other third degree methods were also used. This interrogation lasted continuously from 1800hrs on 8 Jun until approximately 0600hrs on 9 Jun. My body still bears faint scars of this beating.

About 0300 hours on 9 Jun my condition was such that I told my interrogators where I had hidden my parachute. The beating then ceased and apart from being manacled I was reasonably treated. I told my interrogators a partially false story of how, after baling out, I had walked in a certain direction and had been helped by various Frenchmen whose names and addresses I did not know. I was then asked where I had obtained the false identity card which had been found on my person and I stated that it had been brought to me by an unknown Frenchman. My interrogators appeared satisfied that they had succeeded in forcing me to talk by beating me. They also appeared to believe that I was in some way connected with the RAF.

After the interrogation was finished I was taken from CHAMBRAY to a Gestapo HQ in TOURS where I was locked in an unventilated dungeon. My hands were still manacled behind my back. This caused me extreme pain as my shoulder had then been dislocated for 32 days.

At 0100 hours I was taken from the dungeon to an office where I was confronted with another more senior Gestapo interrogator who appeared to specialize in dealing with evading airmen. He began to interrogate me afresh and I repeated my partially untrue story. I maintained this story until midday when the interrogation ceased and I was given a meal but my hands were still manacled.

After I had eaten the meal I was taken to a garage where I saw the French woman who had given me the false identity card and who had escorted F/Sgt FORD and me from RENÉE to BRAIN some 16 days earlier, in a car under guard. She was manacled. I was put into another car and the two cars proceeded in convoy to ANGERS.

On arrival at the SS Headquarters in ANGERS the two cars were parked side by side so that the Frenchwoman and I could see one another.... I remained there as a normal POW for 24 Hours.

About 2300 hours on 10 Jun a Luftwaffe officer took me by car to CHARTRES. On the journey the car broke down and while we were waiting by the roadside for another car, I heard an aircraft, probably a Halifax, circling low in the near distance. Some time later a lorry passed and the occupants fired some shots at us. I am of the opinion that a dropping of arms had taken place in the neighbourhood and this equipment was in the lorry. My escort made no attempt to stop the lorry. Some time later a relief car arrived and I arrived at CHARTRES at about 0800 hours on 11 Jun and was put into solitary confinement in the civil prison. Some time later I discovered that this prison was being used for interrogation purposes by a detachment from the main Luftwaffe interrogation centre at Frankfurt.

I was interrogated at frequent intervals from 11 to 15 Jun by Oberleutenant GABRIELSON, Leutenant Karl SCHMIDT-LUDERS, and Leutenant HORN. I established my identity by giving details of my pre-war career, all of which could be checked from an open RAF list. No pressure was brought to bear when I refused to talk of my activities after 1 Sep 39.

Written interview with Joe Ford. Datelined Tatura, 23 July 1990.

"Q. Did you at any time feel that the difference in rank between you made any intimate exchanges between you and Chaps difficult?

A. No! Emphatically No! When he was brought to the Patard family house at Renée I was thrilled to meet him — that he was alive although severely injured. I called him "Sir" once. He said "I'm known as Chaps and that is it from now on." And it was so. There was no acting in the strong friendship between us. The Ivelaw-Chapman letters and personal visits elevated this friendship far above just good. The British Empire may have faded but it's men of Chaps' breed who gave the world a set of values, expressed or written, for society. And they did it with justice, dignity and humility. What more can you ask of a man?

Q. Do you think Chaps should have been awarded a medal for the way that he kept secret information to himself under interrogation and did he tell you what the secret was.

A. There is no doubt in my mind that a suitable and worthwhile decoration should have been awarded to him. He told me that he had participated in some high level plans covering the invasion of Normandy. It was imperative that he evade capture by the Gestapo. When we were re-united in London after his release he was upset and confessed that he had talked a lot about me under interrogation. In fact he only told them about me after they had this information and I managed to evade capture and continued my escape to England."

Chaps recorded several Anecdotes loosely connected with his interrogation by the Germans. They confirm his remarkable ability to control his mind and his success in outlawing any defeatism even in the most trying circumstances. It must have been this ability to force himself to concentrate on minor details of his surroundings that prevented him from being dominated by his interrogators who were obviously trying to use the shock of his misfortune to prise information from him. Indeed in the case of Schmidt-Luders, he was so far from being dominated that he turned the SS interrogator completely around and made a firm friend of him. There is also evidence of chivalrous behaviour in his treatment by the Germans once he had got out of the hands of the Gestapo.

Biographical Notes. Anecdotes: The Civil Gaol at Chartres.

In June 1944 after I had eventually been freed by the Gestapo I was handed over as a normal POW for interrogation by the Luftwaffe and promptly clapped into Solitary Confinement in a none too salubrious cell of the civil

21. R. I-C when a Prisoner-of-War at Hohemark.

22. '... he held audiences spellbound as he recounted his adventures and experiences' (p.135).

23. *'Mort pour la France et leur Patrie'*. The aircrew grave at St. Rémy du Plain.

24. '... it gave me the opportunity to visit most of the interesting places in the whole sub-continent' (p.145). With the Head Lama, Ladakh, May, 1950.

gaol at Chartres. I don't blame them because I presented them with a bit of a conundrum. I was dressed in an ill-fitting suit of civilian clothes that had belonged to a French farm hand who must have been at least 6 inches shorter than me, and yet I firmly claimed to be an Air Commodore in the Royal Air Force. Since I stuck firmly to the formula of Number Rank and Name, it is no wonder that they kept me in Solitary for a while. Fortunately for me the gaol was in hearing distance of the Cathedral at Chartres whose clock chimes were still functioning. As far as I remember the clock struck the half-hours as well as the hours, and to while away the time I set myself the task, sometimes in total darkness, of trying to estimate the moment of the next chime. At first I was very wide of the mark but after a bit of practice I became quite adept at the game.

Some 2 or 3 months after the War I took Margaret over to meet some of the courageous families who at tremendous risk to themselves had helped me when I was 'On the run'. During our pilgrimage we passed through Chartres so I called at the Civil Gaol. I had a spot of difficulty with the gate porter – I was in Air Vice Marshal's uniform at the time – but eventually I persuaded him to take me to M. Le Commandant's Office. I explained why I was there and said I particularly wanted Margaret to see the cell in which I had done my spell of 'Solitary'. He was most co-operative and entered into the spirit of the mission. He led us off down corridor after corridor of locked cells, occasionally opening one and asking me if that was mine. My recollection of the general layout of the prison was fairly clear and eventually we got on what seemed to me to be familiar ground and right at the end of a long corridor I was able to say to him, "That is the one". The Commandant made the warder get the keys and opened the cell for our full inspection while the two current occupants were made to stand in the corridor, handcuffed to each other.

Biographical Notes. Anecdote; Schmidt-Luders and the Gestapo.

I spent some 7 or 8 months as a POW in a German Hospital near Frankfurt. I was well cared for and as a senior POW Officer for most of the time I had a ward to myself. By this time I had finished with all the unpleasantries of interrogation and was on good terms with Karl Schmidt-Luders, a German Luftwaffe Officer who had first interrogated me when I was in the civil gaol at Chartres. Karl had been at Oxford before the war on exchange from his mother university at Heidelburg. He knew his Shakespeare well and we shared a fondness for such composers as Beethoven, Bach, Brahms and Schubert. Moreover it was plain to me – confidentially – that he had no use for the Nazi regime and was at heart a Liberal in all his thinking and philosophy.

117

My ex-interrogator Karl had not shown up for a while, and I wondered what had happened to him. Actually things had been going pretty badly for the Germans and Karl had been withdrawn from interrogation duties and posted back to a Flak battery in North Italy. He was basically an anti-aircraft weapons officer. At that time Hitler had embarked on his V.1 and V.2 attacks on Great Britain. One night at dinner in his Battery Officer's Mess in Italy the subject of these V weapons cropped up and Karl remarked that he did not consider either of them to be a decisive weapon of war. That remark was overheard by a Mess waiter and was duly reported to the Gestapo. Shortly after Karl was summoned to O.K.V. in Berlin and accused of 'Defeatism'. From then on he was hounded by the Gestapo. I came into the picture because as a side-line he was accused of being too friendly with me. At any rate, not long after, Karl came into my ward, very white about the gills, and told me that the Gestapo were on to him and that they would probably be interrogating me to see what damning evidence they could extract. He begged me to be circumspect in recounting the subjects of any talks I had had with him on the occasions when, several months previously, he had taken me for walks in the Taunus Mountains behind Oberursel. In point of fact the Gestapo did not approach me and Karl apparently weathered the storm as he was still commissioned and taken prisoner by us at the end of the war.

The paradox of this story scarcely needs stressing. At the height of a major war between our two nations, a German Officer was imploring the aid and co-operation of a British Officer who was a prisoner. The situation served as a dire warning to me of the disastrous consequences in lost efficiency if a Secret Police force is implanted in a country's fighting services. Such a situation is unthinkable in the armed forces of the Crown, and long may it be so.

CHAPTER 12

PRISONER OF WAR

A few years after the end of the Second World War, Air Marshal Ivelaw-Chapman and many of his Edwardian Military contemporaries rose to positions of command in the British Armed Forces during the early years of the Cold War. Although his finger was never actually on the nuclear button, as a senior member of the Air Council, his agreement would have been required for a declaration of war. During this time when the Edwardian Military Gentlemen, those who had almost miraculously survived the two World Wars, were in charge of this country's military destiny they brought an admirable degree of wisdom to the task. There were no mad Generals here; no battle-crazed veterans anxious to restart hostilities, any hostilities, in order to recapture the great days of their youth when the war was on. And there was no bitterness and little of the hatred that clouded the military thinking of countries like Israel, and to a lesser extent, the United States.

The Edwardian Military Gentleman seems to have retained throughout his fighting career an admirable tolerance and old-fashioned chivalry that helped him to follow quite sure-footedly the hazardous path of command in the nuclear age.

It is in Chaps' writings from his year as a prisoner that we see evidence of this tolerance and breadth of mind and his awakening conviction that there is always room for humanity in dealing with national enemies. We also see a little of how an Edwardian Gentleman coped with discomfort, ill health and boredom.

When it was confirmed that Chaps was a Prisoner of War in Germany the news was greeted back home with celebration. The uncertainty was over. An announcement was made in *The Times* and telegrams of congratulation arrived on Margaret's doorstep.

Telegram. From Walter Sheen Station Commander Elsham Wolds to Mrs M Ivelaw-Chapman. Cheltenham 2728.

"Heartiest congratulations on best of best news from all at No 13 Base. It shouldn't be long now. Have poured out a strong lemon squash hic on the strength of it. Walter Sheen."

Letter. R I-C to M I-C handwritten in pencil dated 30th June 1944.

"Darling,
This should be the 2nd letter you've had from me. Anyhow, the operation
— a minor- one for a dislocated shoulder has been put off to Tuesday July
4th. What I most want is family news — nothing is too trivial — avoid
anything that might even remotely interest the censor because I'm longing for
your first letter to get through. Next to that is tobacco in sealed tins. Say
it's for POW and they'll know. Could you and Mother send me ½ lb of
Players Medium Navy Cut each alternate fortnight, giving me a sure 1 lb
per month. Assuming that my kit has reached you from my last station, the
next things I would like are nail scissors, 1 pr Baber shoes, medal ribbons
and wings, an india rubber, black shoe polish, pins ordinary, safety and
drawing, ½ yard of rank braid, sewing cotton blue and black, my service
(fore and aft) cap, sock suspenders, braces, a ruler, cuff links, nailbrush,
shaving brush, and a couple of pipes. Please send tobacco separately and
in advance of others. Suggest parcels are not too bulky. I am being well
cared for and have ample freedom in this Sisters of Mercy hospital. So you
have nothing to worry about except to hope for an early end to the War.
God bless you my Darling. I haven't room to say all the things I want but
you know my thoughts are always with you and the children. Kiss them
both from their Daddy. All my Love, C.
PS also please send our old Patience cards and front and back studs.

Journal written during POW captivity. June-October 1944 annotated and
edited, 1946-1951.

For part of the time that I was a POW, I attempted to keep, not exactly a
diary, but a journal that partly records the day to day events but more
generally is comprised of retrospective impressions put to paper two or three
weeks after the event. I was accorded a considerable degree of freedom and
privilege during the time I was in hospital in Frankfurt but my room was
open to search and all my belongings were checked over on more than one
occasion by the Germans. Being anxious to retain this journal long enough
to bring it and the information recorded in code in its pages back to Britain
after the war I was anxious not to record anything that might lead to the
work being confiscated. My notes are therefore slightly coloured in favour
of the regime I was held under.

POW Journal. June 1944

June 10th. Spent day in Luftwaffe barracks at Angers. At 1130 pm set off by car under escort for Chartres. Car broke down but eventually fetched up at Chartres — miserably cold — about 7am. Found myself in a Dulag Luft and was promptly clapped in solitary confinement.

June 11th. In a flea ridden cell of French civil prison in Chartres. Interrogated in evening by three officers. Shaved by a German Corporal with a cut-throat razor. That was brave.

June 12th. In civil prison — solitary confinement.

June 13th. Ditto.

June 14th. Ditto.

June 15th. Released to main prison camp at 8pm.

June 16th. Spent day in main camp amongst seething mass of POWs. Town had been bombed pretty heavily and no water in consequence. Not an attractive spot. Shoulder painful; fleas bad. Think I prefer solitary confinement.

June 17th. Left Chartres Dulag by coach 4am and motored to Gare de L'Est in Paris. Left by train for Frankfurt about 1pm. Reserved compartment in passenger train. Party of 14 plus 4 guards. Rather cold at night but otherwise not bad. Came via Metz and Saarbrucken.

June 18th. Arrived Frankfurt 3am and Dulag Luft at Oberursel at 7am. Clapped into solitary confinement again immediately on arrival. Cell even smaller than Chartres civil gaol. Little sleep as shoulder rather painful. Am anticipating at least ten days of this.

June 19th. Things begin to happen at 10am. I am visited by various officials. Allowed to shave — first for a week; tender enquiries about my shoulder. Visited by a Red Cross official. Am noted down to be visited by the Doctor but before this happens and after the midday meal, an Ober Leutenant Wiebach says that he thinks I will be more comfortable in Hospital. So off we go together to a large private house standing in enormous grounds and I am taken into a large bedroom on the ground floor which is a complete contrast to my various surroundings of last week. First of all a spring bed, the most welcome sight as I am getting an increasing amount of pain from my dislocated shoulder as time goes on. Then sheets, actually sheets; an orderly to bring my food which is no longer prison fare, but four meals a day and quite ample in quality and quantity. Hot and cold water laid on in the bedroom and a reading lamp by the bed. English books are brought and although I am still, strictly speaking, in solitary confinement, I spend the first really comfortable night since I left England, despite my shoulder giving rather a lot of trouble.

June 20th. Into Frankfurt by ambulance for X-Ray, accompanied by the Doctor who looks after POW patients and who, though only 36, is reputed to be one of the best orthopaedic surgeons in Germany. Modern hospital, beautifully laid out and very reminiscent of the Westminster. X-Ray shows

a very bad dislocation and the Doctor warns me that there is little
likelihood (after 6 weeks) that he can restore to normal. He consults with
the Chief Surgeon of the Frankfurt hospital and they decide not to operate
till next Tuesday to give me time to recover from my recent solitary
confinement. They expect to leave the shoulder where it is since it is too
late to restore to normal position, but by cutting away bone of the humerus
they will restore to me about half the movement of the left arm. In the
evening I was visited by a Welfare Officer – a Hauptman of the
Luftwaffe – who was in the last war. He brought a bottle of the best
Hock, part of which we consumed together, the remainder being left with
me to drink in my own time. Am being made to feel thoroughly
comfortable and at ease, but still no sign of the real business which is
final interrogation.

There is a lot of double talk here as each side tries to out-think the other. Chaps is still defensive against interrogation. He probably thinks that the sudden switch to kindly treatment is part of the classic 'Nice man, Nasty man' interrogator's play. He therefore mistrusts his captors but doesn't say so in the journal because he knows it is not secure. The Germans, all but the Gestapo, know that the War is lost and feel the cold wind of War Crimes Trials blowing towards them. Some good press from a senior British prisoner in the form of a private journal will do them no harm and there is the possibility that Chaps, imagining his notes to be private and his codes un-cracked, will slip up and reveal something to his diary that he would never have revealed under interrogation. As a witness to how he was treated, and who did what to him personally the journal must be considered unreliable, but as a testimony to the honour and humanity of the German medical staff at Hohemark and Oberursel it can not fail to amaze.

POW Journal. Extracts.

July 1st. The only day of note amongst these five was Sunday when I
was lent a suit of civilian clothes, shades of peacetime England, and at
9am Wiebach and I, both clad in mufti, left here to go to church in the
town of Oberursel about 3 miles away. The church itself requires no
description since it was relatively modern and rather severe in its
simplicity but by no means devoid of an atmosphere of reverence and
worship. The service, being Lutheran, was simple and unadorned and
although I could understand nothing of his sermon, the Pastor, on
Wiebach's interpretation after the service had preached a helpful sermon
on the theme of the path to God being strewn with hardship. That his

subject was at least topical was evidenced by the amount of mourning amongst the congregation. At least 75% of the women were in black.

Readers may note a marked change in the style of Chaps' written prose in the POW Journal. "That his subject was at least topical was evidenced by the amount of mourning" is not what he would have written before the War. He was reading extensively from the Hohemark library almost to the extent of giving himself a degree course in English literature and as each book was completed he wrote a concise and erudite criticism of the work as he saw it. These reviews were all carefully typed up when he came home and pasted in the scrap book but who did he imagine would read them? One can only conclude that while he was a prisoner he read and reviewed these numerous great works of literature not for pleasure alone but to exercise his brain and to keep at bay the boredom which he so much despised. And if he devoured a work of Dickens in a couple of days, we can not be surprised if the occasional Dickensian phrase creeps into his writing.

Literary Criticisms. Written 1944 when Prisoner of War.

Having just finished David Copperfield, I can't refrain from making a note of criticism of what is generally recognized as one of Dickens' masterpieces. There is no denying the human touch with which the various characters are drawn, nor the simplicity which makes the story so readable and gives life to the large circle of people who we meet in its pages; but I was left with the strong impression that Dickens, in this instance, has stretched his net too wide in presenting to the reader within the compass of one narrative so vast and varied a mixture of personalities. So diverse are these characters in personality, walk of life, age and profession that the author has to resort to a number of different artifices in order to keep them within the framework of the main story.

There is a distinct touch of artificiality about little Miss Mowcher the dwarf being concerned in the eventual arrest of Mr Littimer; he stretches our credulity to the utmost when he allows the rivals James Steerforth and Ham Peggoty to meet their deaths on the same night, in the same tempest and even in the same bit of ocean, when their paths have not crossed for a matter of years.

Galsworthy takes on a no less difficult task in holding together the great diversity of characters in the Forsyte Saga, but in my appreciation he achieves his aim with no apparent trace of artifice.

And while Chaps was making a determined effort to exercise his intellect by reading Dickens, the Bible and Galsworthy, the admirable Dr Ittershagen was working miracles on the dislocated shoulder.

POW Journal. July 4th — July 11th 1944.

*I have just returned to Hohemark after having spent a week in the basement
ward of the Luftwaffe Hospital in Frankfurt.*

*It seems as if the operation itself was much more successful than the doctors
expected remembering that the dislocation was now 60-days old and the arm
quite useless. Having opened up the shoulder joint Dr Ittershagen (the 36
year old orthopaedic surgeon with a growing reputation throughout
Germany), discovered that he could get the arm to go back in its socket after
all; a fact about which there was considerable doubt from the X-Ray photo.
However, as soon as he had got the joint back in, it sprang out again,
pulled by one of the muscles which got misplaced during the long period of
dislocation. So he proceeded to cut into that muscle and that had the desired
effect of making the arm joint stay put in its proper place. He then sewed
up the muscle again in its new position and having fixed up the rest of the
ligaments and whatnots, sealed up the incision.*

*The Op. took 38 minutes and I woke up in my ward without any sickness
at all and with no very acute pain. My shoulder was in plaster and the
whole arm bandaged to a wire-work frame affair which allowed no
movement whatsoever.*

*I think there can scarcely be a moment when inability to speak the local
language can be more distressing than in the first 6 to 8 hours after coming
round from an operation performed in a foreign country. I couldn't help but
be amused by the efforts of the German nurses as they tried to make me
understand their questions. Did I want the 'Bottle', Morphia or a sleeping
draft?*

Biographical Notes. Anecdote. Dr Ittershagen and 'His' Shoulder.
Written 1968.

*After some delay Dr Ittershagen the orthopaedic surgeon at Oberursel Dulag
and I together with the X-Ray photographs of my shoulder were summoned
into the presence of the head surgeon of the hospital, a Colonel. This officer
showed me from the photographs that my humerus was now some 2 inches
below its socket in the scapula. He explained that the only solution was a
graft which, though depriving me of rotation, would still leave me with
most other shoulder movement. Whereupon Ittershagen — a mere Captain
in rank — clicked his heels and said "Sir, I would like to operate on the
Air Commodore because I think I could restore rotation of the shoulder
despite the 2 months' dislocation." There ensued quite a lengthy argument*

which I was unable to follow, but in the end Ittershagen was permitted, somewhat patronizingly, to have a go. He operated and after one or two unsuccessful attempts he managed to get the humerus back into its socket with a reasonable chance of staying there.

The operation was 100% successful and from that day to this I have never lost full rotation of my arm and still retain practically full movement of my shoulder.

Ittershagen naturally was delighted with his success and we became firm friends. He wrote an article about it describing the technique he used during the operation which was published in the German equivalent of the Lancet.

Soon after the war I ferreted out Ittershagen, then back in civil practice in Frankfurt. I had scarcely entered his flat before he peeled off my jacket and shirt with the words, "And how is MY shoulder?" That has been his greeting too on the many later occasions when I have met him.

In view of the extraordinary depth of his experience, Chaps was regularly asked in the years after his retirement, for his advice on many subjects. He was unusually humble as a counsellor and often would decline, stating that he didn't feel qualified to express an opinion at all. However, on the subject of Depression he was quite forthright and regularly came out with the rather blimpish opinion that depression was a state of mind rather than a definable illness and that most depression was self-curable using a well defined set of procedures. A critic might have felt that he and his generation were unsympathetic towards clinical depression because the circumstances of their lives shielded them from ever suffering from it. Not so; a drug-induced depression while recovering from surgery was one of the greatest problems that Chaps had to deal with during his incarceration.

POW Journal for July 16–August 26 1944.

On Friday 21st the Doctor took out the second and supposedly the last set of stitches. That night I had a rotten bad night and much pain from the wound and the next day the Doctor, after digging round inside, found an internal stitch that had not dissolved and he removed it. I was glad that he had found the root of the trouble and imagined that from then on all would go swimmingly, but actually it proved to be the start of quite a serious relapse which lasted six weeks.

The wound turned septic internally and the poison spread all along the shoulder. I ran a high fever and pus poured out of the wound and leaked through the bandages and on to the pillow. I had rotten nights with sometimes only a couple of hours sleep. The Doctor put me on Sulphanilamide B.P. (Which I regarded as the same as our own M and B

*though it was not the kind that was a recognized cure for pneumonia) My
pulse went low, my joints were hot and at night my feet and hands swelled
up to an alarming size. Obviously my heart was affected and for a fortnight
the Doctor had to give me daily injections of some stuff called Dexterpura
to boost the action of my heart. On one occasion he took my blood pressure
which at my age should be 100/145 and found it to be 60/100.*

*In the meantime I felt pretty cheap and miserable. I lost all energy and
to some extent my vitality. I felt quite worn out by the short journey up a
short flight of stairs from my bedroom to the Bandage Room where the
Doctor changed my dressings. In addition as a result of the M and B I lost
my palate and my appetite and got occasional attacks of nausea. At one time
I could not keep down solid food and lived on soup only. To cap everything
was the depression caused by the M and B. I was taking 5 tablets a day of
5 grammes and took them for over a fortnight.*

POW book review. *On Being a Real Person* — H.E. Fosdick. Written in
1944.

*This book amounts to a treatise on the relation between psychiatry and real
religion. Amongst other things the author deals with all the human emotions
such as jealousy, fear, depression, anxiety etc. and the chapter which
impressed me most was the one dealing with depression, for which he offers
six antidotes:*

    i. Take depression for granted.

    *ii. We should identify ourselves not with our worse but with our better
moods.*

    *iii. When depression comes a man should tackle himself and not merely
blame the circumstances.*

    iv. Remember others.

    v. In any depressing situation a man should look for possibilities.

    *vi. A man should remember that some tasks are so important that they
must be carried out irrespective of any depression that may overtake him.*

But the infection finally cleared, the M and B — the first of the anti-biotics
— was suspended and the black depressions overcome. Chaps saw out most
of the rest of his time as a Prisoner at the Oberursel Hospital. He seems to
have been retained at the main reception and interrogation centre for allied
aircrew and not sent on to a normal prisoner of war camp partly because of
his unusual seniority and partly because of the interest taken in his medical
progress by Dr Ittershagen. He made no attempt to escape largely because
of his physical condition and also because the War was clearly coming to an
end. He first records hearing the sound of heavy artillery in September, 1944.

The extracts from his journal that follow are selected for the light they throw on the development of his character during a period which had much in common with a compulsory sojourn in a religious retreat. It was here that he espoused humility, stepped back from the arrogance of command and, with the enthusiasm of a true Christian optimist, he sought out the best in his fellow men.

POW Journal. Entry for 12 July 1944.

.... perhaps a word or two of further description might not be amiss concerning Hohemark which I had previously termed a Hospital but which should probably be termed a Home. It is a curious fact that on this, the second occasion in my career that I have been made Prisoner of War — the first being in 1929 in Afghanistan — I have again fetched up in a Haven of Rest where religion is the predominant feature. From one aspect I can not help likening this place to the Pir Sahib's Fort outside Jellalabad where I enjoyed a fortnight of his hospitality and the security his position gave me, in the midst of warring tribesmen. The attraction of this place Hohemark is in its many aspects: military, civil and POW. Actually in peacetime it was a large nursing home for neurotic cases, standing in its own park and established, I should imagine as a speculation, by three Frankfurt Doctors. As things are now, the predominant partners are the German Army who run it as a convalescent home for their shell-shock cases throughout Germany, but there are still a large number of mainly aged civil patients as well as anything up to 70 British and American POWs. But the curious point about the whole strange admixture is that from the nursing aspect the hospital is run by a religious order of Lutheran Sisters of Mercy. By and large one could not expect ever to come across a more disparate fusion of thoughts and ideas under one roof. However, it all seems to work out very well and the Holy Sisters do not seem to be unduly worried by the burly German military guards who prowl around outside the building to see that no one escapes. The Sisters also seem to exercise a calming influence here. The Americans stop their almost constant swearing in their presence, and no prisoner suffers interrogation of any sort while suffering from wounds or injuries.

September 24th to October 18th 1944.

These last three or four weeks have been one long process of recuperation as far as my arm is concerned. By dint of diathermic treatment and a set of self-designed exercises which I perform three times daily, my arm and shoulder muscles on the left side are showing definite signs of revival. My achievements to date include putting my hand in my trouser pocket, reaching my left eyebrow with my thumb, shaving (Downwards only) my left cheek and walking up and down my room 30 times carrying a 4 lb weight slung from my left hand. In spite of this improvement I am getting more and more dejected as I have not yet heard from Margaret...

Another little amenity of this Hospital lies in the matter of hair-cutting. Every 10 days or so I get my hair trimmed by a German medical orderly who still owns his own barber shop in Chicago. He does my hair every bit as well as Reed at the RAF Club...

I have taken it upon myself to look after the library in the men's ward upstairs. It doesn't involve much work but I like to have some specific daily job. I also wash up for the staff table and do all my own laundry. In India I would have combined the roles of Dhobi wallah and Masalchi...

At 2.30 in the afternoon which is coffee and bread and jam time − I leave my room on the ground floor and have the rest of my meals with the British and American medical orderlies and Dr Ittershagen who feeds with us. I spend the rest of the day with the other prisoners − 75% American and 25% RAF − all of whom are to a greater or lesser degree wounded and I do what little I can do to help out in the running of the place, which is really a casualty clearing station for British and American prisoners of war. This has greatly aroused my interest and I have been able to study the psychological difference between the American and the Englishman in adversity. I have also seen some pitiable sights in the way of burned, maimed and wounded aircrew and seen at close hand some of the more gruesome horrors of war. Dr Ittershagen is humane to a degree and treats each man as a 'Case', irrespective of rank, class, nationality or creed. He even seems to pay extra attention to the quite numerous Jews which are amongst the Americans just to show his strict impartiality.

Another great advantage I have derived from mixing in with the other prisoners is to get a proper sense of proportion in regard to my own, relatively light suffering.

I can not finish this short review of Hohemark Reserve Lazarett without a short mention of Stanley. Stanley was a Sergeant Air Gunner in the RAF, shot down and badly wounded some three years ago. He has taught himself the job of medical orderly with such success that he is now an indispensable part of this hospital and is trusted and relied on by Ittershagen to dress some of the worst wounds that come in here. While the Doctor was on leave I watched Stanley handle amputations and gunshot wounds with the confidence and efficiency of a qualified man. He works sometimes for 14 hours at a stretch when a big batch of wounded comes in.

The next extract which concerns a major operation that Chaps witnessed in the Frankfurt Hospital illustrates well how a man's experiences can colour his opinions at any stage of his life. Chaps' generation had a resistance to propaganda that made them take with scepticism any suggestion that behaviour patterns were a factor of race. He learnt at Hohemark that the evils of Nazism were by no means universal in Germany and that it was unsafe to imagine therefore, that all Germans were evil. While at home, at the time of the bombing of Dresden, there was a much publicized feeling that "The only good German was a dead German", Chaps was finding out with certainty that there were convincing exceptions to this rule.

When he witnessed the pinning of a leg in Frankfurt Hospital, the guns of the advancing Allies could already be heard in the City. Hamburg had been fire-bombed. The horrors of some of the Concentration Camps had already been uncovered, and another German Doctor was practising unspeakable genetic experiments on pairs of Jewish twins in Auschwitz. Chaps himself had been tortured as had his French Resistance guide. His protector in France had been shot down in cold blood and Gestapo snoopers were everywhere. These surely were the circumstances in which we could expect bitterness and recrimination to be rife and every man to turn against his neighbour. Yet here is Dr Ittershagen performing a complicated operation on an enemy airman; surgery that wasn't by any stretch of the imagination vital but which was designed to ensure that in old age the patient would not be impeded by a stiff leg and probably arthritis.

The story is one that Chaps often told. He was enormously impressed by the simple mechanics of the surgery and by the confidence in the future that it portrayed.

POW Journal. August 1944.

The main interest that I got from my visit to Frankfurt Hospital was to witness a complete operation from first incision to final stitch. Ittershagen was operating on an American POW whose thigh bone had been badly set in some Belgian hospital by a Polish surgeon. He had been left with a stiff leg which was a few centimetres shorter than the other. Ittershagen did one of his pinning jobs — a relatively new technique of which he is one of the leading exponents in Europe.

First of all he cut into the leg, re-broke the bone and cleaned up the two damaged ends. The lower part of the limb, now attached only by skin and muscle was pushed away to one side on a separate trolley. Then, working more like a blacksmith than a surgeon he set to work with a heavy hammer to drive a two foot steel rod from the hip joint, down the inside of the upper thigh bone. When the rod reached the broken end, the lower limb was matched up with the upper part and the steel rod driven right through the centre thus uniting the thigh bone. The wound was then sewn up. The fellow will be walking normally with the steel rod inside the bone in about 4 weeks' time, and in five months the rod will be removed and the space filled up with marrow. I have never seen an op. before and I was thoroughly intrigued, not least by the speed at which he worked. He did the whole job in thirty minutes and it was an education to watch the proceedings.

During the whole of his time at the interrogation centre and in the hospital at Hohemark, Chaps was Senior Allied Officer and in spite of the somewhat lowly tasks which he chose to undertake he made sure that his seniority was unmistakable. He also accepted unquestioningly the responsibilities of his position even when his own physical condition was at its lowest ebb.

Letter written to Lt Cdr J.R. Suffren, (Royal Australian Navy) Ballarat, Victoria, Australia.

"From; Air Commodore R. Ivelaw-Chapman, RAF.
Hohemark Kurhaus
  Oberursel
   Frankfurt.

Dear Commander Suffren,
  You will probably have heard by now, through the Red Cross or from official sources, that your brother, Ted, died at 5.10 pm yesterday in this reserve hospital at Hohemark which is some 12 miles from Frankfurt-am -Main in south west Germany. Knowing how bald and comfortless are these official notifications I thought you might like to hear more of how Ted met his end. But first let me introduce myself. I am the senior British prisoner of war patient in the same hospital where Ted died and have been here for about 10 months.
  I first met your brother when he was in the large German Luftwaffe hospital in Frankfurt itself. He had been severely wounded when he first baled out in Denmark last April and he was in hospital there for 2 or 3 months. I was immediately attracted to him by his fine spirit and his philosophical attitude to his wounds. A large splinter of metal had penetrated his back and pierced his bladder, and there were other injuries as well. The German Doctors and Nurses fought hard for him and I can assure you they did as much for him as they would have done for one of their own fellows. They operated on him several times for the succession of stones which kept forming in his kidneys and did their best to stop the spread of urosepsis which is an almost inevitable concomitant to bladder wounds. They gave

him several blood transfusions to try and build up his strength, but all to no avail.

Eventually when there was definitely no hope of recovery I persuaded the German Doctors to let him be moved from the large hospital in Frankfurt where he was in a small basement ward below street level because of the bombing, out to this pleasant haven of rest. Here there are sunshine, trees and blue sky for outlook and 70-odd British and American patients and a number of RAAF boys who used to chat to him about home. His spirit to the last was of the finest and all who came in contact with him had the greatest respect for his courage and the fight for life that he put up. He is being buried tomorrow in a small township called Oberursel about 4 miles from here and in a pleasant cemetery.

I would like to mention one more fact. A Second Lieutenant of the United States Air Force, one Beauregard by name, who hails from New York was Ted's constant friend for the last 6 months of his life. His devotion to Ted and his unceasing care and sickroom attention to him was one of the finest sights I have seen in this war. Your brother was a fine chap and a grand example of the best Australian manhood. God rest his Soul.

Yours Sincerely
R. Ivelaw-Chapman.

On 19 March, 1945 Chaps, along with the Kommandant and Staff of the Dulag Luft at Oberursel were moved rearwards to a Camp at Buchenbuhl. The advancing Americans were not far behind them. Oberursel was liberated on 27 March.

MI9 Debriefing Form. Dated 19th April 1945.

On 19th March I was taken by Bus to Buchenbuhl where I arrived on 20th March. I remained there till the arrival of American Forces at 1700 hours on 16th April when I handed over the Camp Commandant Ober-Leutenant Killinger and approximately 200 German guards as POWs to 45 Division US Army. Before leaving I obtained a safe conduct for the German medical orderlies to bring in German wounded and dead from the local battle. After being liberated I travelled by Jeep to a Battalion HQ at Behringersdorf where I gave local tactical information to the Bn. Commander. I was then conveyed by jeep to 45 Divn. HQ at Lauf where I spent the night.

Biographical Notes. Anecdotes. A Needless Question.

In April 1945 after having been a Prisoner of War for close on a year I was liberated by American Forces who overran the particular POW Camp near Nuremberg where I had been for the past month. I got hold of a US Major and told him that I would like to get back to England pretty quickly. "That's OK, Buddy," he told me, "I'll get you transportation to a repatriation unit and you'll be back home within ten days or a fortnight." That was not my idea at all and I explained to him that despite the semi-civilian kit that I was wearing at the time I was in fact an Air Commodore and I persuaded him to give me a Jeep to the nearest airstrip. Here I asked a US Colonel whether he had anything going to England that day. "No," he answered, "but I've got a DC3 coming in this afternoon. It's not going straight to England. Would I mind going via Paris?" Would I mind a night in Paris after a year 'In the Bag', I ask you!

Anecdote. Christmas 1944.

I spent Christmas 1944 in the hospital attached to Dulag Luft, just outside Frankfurt which was the main interrogation centre for all captured allied airmen. Part of the layout of the Dulag Luft consisted of some 100 to 120 solitary confinement cells (one of which I occupied for a bit) where POWs were incarcerated as a matter of routine before and during their interrogation by German intelligence experts before being sent on to ordinary POW camps scattered about Germany.

By Christmas 1944 the Germans, or at least the more intelligent amongst them, knew full well that they had been defeated. One German interrogator – Dr Karl Schmidt-Luders whom I got to know well both during and after the War when we exchanged social visits on more than one occasion, told me they were making a special effort to avoid having anybody actually in Solitary on Christmas Day. However, they failed by one.... a certain Flight Lieutenant whose name I never discovered was the sole occupant of that long corridor of cells. Schmidt-Luders decided to take this officer for a walk on Christmas afternoon. The prisoner had made his routine visit to the 'Abort' in the morning and when Schmidt-Luders arrived in his cell in the afternoon he found it festooned with paper chains of loo paper and the walls decorated with the cheerful message...."A HAPPY CHRISTMAS TO ME."

The Wuppertal Trial and its Sequel.

I would like to try and recapture the scene in the courtroom at Wuppertal on November 26th 1945.

The big war-criminal trial at Nuremberg has just begun. The exposure of the horrors perpetrated at Belsen and Buchenwald have stunned the world. The evidence of returning POWs has given rise to a number of War Criminal Trials at various places, concerned with varying degrees of German brutality. In the courtroom at Wuppertal the atmosphere is tense. The court is composed of British and American senior officers. A British Judge Advocate General is there to direct the court on procedure and an American legal officer is the prosecutor. The Press of many nations are present in court. The indictment is read out; that of overheating solitary confinement cells to unbearable levels in order to extract information from prisoners at Germany's main interrogation centre; the Dulag Luft outside Frankfurt. A string of POWs come forward to testify. Everybody is in uniform including myself as an Air Vice Marshal (Senior, I think, to the President of the Court).

I was absorbed by the proceedings and seated in the 'Public Gangway'. The Judge Advocate addressed the court and said that he understood that there was a person in the court-room who was later to be called to give evidence. This he said was most irregular. The President asked if there was any such person in the room and I stood up. "You expect to be called later for the Prosecution?" asked the President. "No," I replied, "For the Defence." My words, I modestly admit, galvanized the courtroom.

As a result of my testimony some of the accused were acquitted but Oberst Killinger, the Dulag Luft Commandant was sentenced to 5 years' imprisonment. He, in fact, pleaded guilty as he was the commanding officer when the cell-roasting incident took place though I am convinced it was without his knowledge.

Later I discovered that he was in a civil gaol at Werl in Germany. I was AOC No 38 Group at the time and more or less free to fly where I would over Europe. I waited a month or so after the trial and then, equipped with an adequate supply of cigarettes, chocolate, a bottle of whisky and plenty of coffee which I knew meant so much to the Germans I flew to the nearest airfield and then motored to the prison. I found that the Governor was a German civilian and not a generous man. Yes, Killinger was in his gaol; Yes, I could see him for a few minutes but no, I could leave him no comforts. The rules did not permit it.

I told the story to the German driver who drove me back to the airfield. He wasn't surprised. "That is why you won the war," he said. "The British know how to bend the rules. The Germans obey the letter of the law till the last man is shot."

His grasp of his own national characteristics surprised me as much as his perfect English, but in immediate post-war Germany you never knew who might be driving your car. The man was probably a university professor.

Examination of the Ivelaw-Chapman Visitors' Book for the period 1947 to

1949 when the family resided in the AOC's Residence, Littlecote House, Enford, Wiltshire, shows several visits from German residents domiciled in the area of Frankfurt-am-Main: Dr. Ittershagen, Karl Schmidt-Luders and ultimately, after 3 years' incarceration in his own country, Otto Killinger.

CHAPTER 13

POSTWAR

Chaps came home from the war in reasonable health and rejoicing in his survival. For a while he held audiences spellbound as he recounted his experiences and adventures, but only for a few weeks did he allow himself to think about the momentous events of the previous eighteen months. Soon he was a working Royal Air Force Officer again and looking for the next job to do and the next aeroplane to fly. For those who were near him, he was infuriatingly reticent about what had actually happened. The family only heard of the Gestapo torture many years later from war books and newspaper reports, and the matter of the D-Day secrets was never aired until after his death.

His stories and adventures in the immediate postwar period show magnanimity rather than bitterness and simple gratitude as opposed to any desire for vengeance. Although he was now aged 47 and slightly incapacitated by his damaged shoulder and a postwar injury to his back, he never considered retirement.

There are no records concerning senior military reaction to his slight indiscretion with regard to the secret invasion plans. He was neither court martialled for endangering security nor decorated for successfully maintaining it. It is safe to assume that the former was traded off against the latter. Winston Churchill certainly expressed his gratitude directly to Chaps and we can assume that the two men agreed to share the secret on an 'All's Well that Ends Well' understanding. The two men were certainly closer in the 1950s than would normally be expected in a relationship between the Prime Minister and a fairly junior member of the Air Council.

Anecdote; The Phone Call. Ivelaw-Chapman Folklore.

During Churchill's postwar premiership the Ivelaw-Chapman family lived in a large flat on Putney hill. On an undistinguished Sunday afternoon in 1952 the telephone rang and a junior member of the family answered it. The voice at the other end was unmistakable; the gruff delivery, the orator's pauses, the crushed r sounds and the words that seemed to erupt from the depths of the old man's stomach:

"Ask Sir Ronald if he'd be good enough to have a word with me; ... it's

Ten Downing Street here." It was, of course, impossible to hear much of the conversation but it can be reported that the Prime Minister called Sir Ronald 'Chaps' and there was every indication that he had rung up for little more than a chat with an old friend.

Chaps made several visits to France after the war to renew acquaintance with the people of St Rémy du Plain and the villages along his escape route who had helped him in 1944. They treated him as a returning hero, a sentiment which always surprised him. "Anyone might think," he would say, "that I had risked my life for them and not the other way round." It is quite clear from reading the letters and journals of the participants in Chaps' 1944 evasion in France that even when he was shocked and frightened and on the run; when he was dressed in dirty and ill-fitting clothes and when his command of the language was little better than that of a schoolboy, he dazzled those around him with the sheer force of his personality. Like those who knew him in Afghanistan and in India they realized that out of the sky had fallen no ordinary man. The story of his sojourn with them began straightaway to pass into folklore exactly as it had done in the Pir Sahib's sanctuary and there is no indication that the good people of St Rémy and the other villages will ever forget him. And his feelings for them were every bit as warm, respectful and indeed loving. The comradeship of adversity shared is a powerful force and easily transcends the short-lived differences which politicians try to force between the common men of separate nations.

Biographical Notes. Anecdotes. The Uniform.

As soon as I got back into a position where I could command an aeroplane again I set off in a Lysander for St Rémy du Plain accompanied by Walter Sheen who commanded Elsham Wolds when I went Missing. The object of the visit was to meet old friends, but mainly to recover my battledress uniform which I had handed over to a French woman as soon as I made contact with the Resistance. The warmth of their welcome quite overcame me. It was as though I personally had saved them and their village from Nazi domination and not the opposite. Although few of my immediate helpers had actually suffered on my behalf the risks that they ran were enormous. The local Priest who officiated at the burial of the rest of my crew was a member of the Resistance and died in a concentration camp.

The battledress was buried in the garden of one of my helpers in St Rémy. (Note how reluctant he is even after the war to reveal names and exact locations.) *We went exactly to the spot and the woman herself,* with some assistance started to dig furiously. At a depth of about 3 feet a wooden box was located and inside, carefully wrapped in oilskin was my battledress. It was perfectly dry and ready to wear, but they insisted on taking it away to be cleaned while we partook of a small celebratory lunch. Also carefully stored in the underground hiding place was my penknife and the small change from my pockets and amazingly the laundry marks, labels and a few Cash's name tags that we had removed from my shirt, socks and underwear.

After lunch which was lavish and considerably more alcoholic than either Walter Sheen or I with an aeroplane to fly home could do justice to, the newly cleaned and pressed uniform was handed over. My hosts had heard of my impending promotion and on the jacket they had added a very fair approximation of the extra ring of an Air Vice Marshal.

I was put under immense pressure to return to St Rémy and naturally I promised to do so.

Biographical Notes. Visit to Paris 18 July 1945.

At the end of July 1945 (Only 6 weeks after the end of the War) I was sent by the Air Ministry to Paris in order to advise on what steps should be taken to set up a Franco-British Association that would be a permanent link between RAF and Dominion Airmen and the individual French men and women who helped them to evade or escape. There evolved from my report what is now known as the RAF Escaping Society. The general purpose behind this society follows to a large degree my original suggestions, particularly the stated purpose of arranging for annual meetings between individual French helpers and those men in this country whom they made such sacrifices for. Later when we are all old, grey and infirm we shall begin to dispense charity, but initially it is the spirit of mutual respect and support that must not be allowed to fade away.

Biographical Notes. Anecdotes. The Bottle of Calvados.

About 3 months after Hitler's war was over, with some difficulty I got permission from the Air Ministry to take Margaret over to France in a service aircraft (D.H. Dragon Rapide) flown by myself. The purpose was to visit some of the many other families who had helped me out when I was on the run in France during the war. Our first port of call was St Rémy du Plain where we were guests of the Mayor, M.Thibault, in the Moulin, a small château just outside the village. It was within a mile or two of the spot where I first touched terra firma when I baled out from a Lancaster in May 1944.

It is not difficult to imagine the warmth of the occasion with its successions of 'Vins d'honneur', 'Banquets de reunion', and endless other signs of welcome to the 'Maréchal de l'Air' whom they had only known as a rather frightened 'Evader' 18 months previously and for whom they had literally risked their lives.

Some details of this delightful, crowded and in a way sentimental visit are now fading from my memory, but one event stands out well in my mind. At the final dinner, for 30-odd, in the château, I mentioned to M. Thibault my appreciation of the Calvados that was being served as a liqueur after dinner. That night, before Margaret and I retired to bed, M. Thibault sent to his cellar for a carafe of Calvados − possibly one of his most cherished possessions − labelled in pencil with the date of his marriage, 1888. He insisted on giving it to me. The contents are long gone but the carafe I still have and greatly treasure.

Letter from Margaret Ivelaw-Chapman to a friend. August 14th 1945. Written from the depths of austerity Britain where a week's butter ration would not be enough for a single jacket potato, a banana was an unknown wonder and no one remembered what Champagne tasted like.

"My Dear Willoughby,

I feel our experience last week will interest you enough to warrant a full description of it. Chaps received an invitation from the Mayor of the village of St Rémy du Plain − the village where he was first picked up in May 1944 − to take part in the celebrations on the anniversary of their liberation and to be the guest of honour...

"As we drove into St Rémy many of the villagers were out to greet us and when we arrived at the Mayor's Château the whole family were at the door. It is a wonderful old place − 14th century. They gave us a terrific welcome, much kissing of Chaps and hand shakes and we were given a huge bedroom up an old spiral staircase. No one could speak English. We arrived about 7pm, very hungry, but there seemed no sign of food and more and more people arrived; hundreds of relations and a party of travelling players who were also staying in the Moulin. At last, at 10pm, when we had given up hope of a meal, an aperitif arrived − very good wine. Then we went into the dining room to find a veritable banquet laid for 25 people and we sat down to a nine-course meal that lasted for 3 hours. There were 6 different wines including Champagne and liqueurs. At 1.30 the players started performing; singing, piano, violin, comic turns. We finally got to bed at 3.30 in the morning − dead beat. The next morning we had to assemble at 9.30 and set off for the village where we found everyone outside the Mayor's parlour. Chaps had to shake hands with all the councillors and the Old Soldiers and then we processed to the church where there was a Mass and blessing of a memorial flag. The four corners of the flag were held by a French soldier of the First World War, one of this war, a member of the Resistance and a British officer.

"Then we processed to the War Memorial where a wreath was laid and the names of the fallen read out and then we marched behind a band of trumpets and drums to the cemetery where we had a little service round the grave of the other 5 members of Chaps' aircraft who were killed. It is kept most beautifully and always has flowers. Chaps made a speech in French and the Mayor read out the names of the English airmen. It was all very moving and I didn't dare think too much of the significance of that grave.

"Then we processed back to the village where we sat down 135-strong to another banquet...There was much health drinking and speechifying.... Whenever we arrived anywhere or departed they struck up God Save the Queen...

One of the funniest moments came when Madame le Mayor took me over the road to the back yard of a pub and there was a queue of women waiting outside the Loo. I was solemnly introduced and shook hands with the queue and then Madame lead me to the front and held open the door for me to enter while the whole queue smiled and waved. It was a filthy dirty place too...

"M. le Mayor offered me his arm for a walk round the field and we fetched up at a sort of buffet and I felt that a cup of tea would be most welcome — but oh no! Champagne once more... in the middle of the afternoon...

"Chaps and I hurried off because we were anxious to go and explore the countryside. We went with the son and daughter in law who had looked after him to the field where he was first seen getting a drink and we found the bramble bush where he had hidden all day. Then we went to another farm where he had stayed and met the Patard family. The grandmother, son, daughter in law and little Jean-Pierre aged 6. There we also met Jacques, the man who more or less ran the Resistance Movement in that area. He was a terrific character and I could imagine him doing anything. We went up to the attic where Chaps lived for ten days unbeknown to most of the family and where he played with the child's Meccano set. They still have the bridge intact that he made during those days. We had another huge meal there and talked over the old days. We got back to the Mayor's house to find them still eating...

"We meant to leave at 7.30am. When we got downstairs the whole family was there with flowers and a bottle of Calvados and there had to be more photographs and, just as we were about to leave, more Champagne!!! at 8 o'clock in the morning.

"Their farewells were most touching and they made us promise to come back again next year and bring the children. As we drove through the village there were many out to wave us goodbye and we felt we had left a lot of true friends....I have never seen such hospitality and kindness....They seem to regard Chaps as their special property and were so grateful to him for coming. Of course all the gratitude should be on our side.

We are off to Cornwall on the 29th for 2 weeks,

Yours as Ever,
Margaret."

Written interview with Joe Ford; July 1990.

"We have been able to maintain a very close relationship with the French families who gave Chaps and me shelter, acted as guides and who took incredible risks to ensure my safe return to the UK. My wife is fond of writing letters and her complete dedication to this work has been a vital plank which must never be underestimated. Furthermore she made personal visits with me in 1965, 1969, and 1973.

"Our son Paul and his wife Louise welded a new link in March 1988. They were able to visit our known helpers, some of them now more than 80 years old.

"I have lived 75 years in a remarkable period. My war service gave me many bonuses. I met my wife. I met Chaps. I learnt many things; to be a good listener; to accept rapid change. You asked me if after nearly 50 years I considered my war experience to be basically a good or a bad thing. I don't know. There are six crosses at Bayeux cemetery [The common grave of the aircrew lost in the crash of Chaps' Lancaster was moved from St Rémy Churchyard to a British military cemetery at Bayeux.] it could so easily have been 7 or 8. Why did we survive? Have we fulfilled the privilege? I don't know but I am certain that the links of wartime friendship that unite our 3 countries should be maintained for as long as men still tell stories of long ago wars.

Letter from Madame Guéhenno, née Annie Rospabe once known as Gilberte, to Margaret Ivelaw-Chapman. Dated January 1991. Both ladies are now widows.

"My Dear Margaret,

Thank-you very much for your letter, I received many many days ago — please excuse me. I was very busy these last weeks... we say in French "Le diable est pavé de bonnes intentions." I am very happy to know that everything is going well with you and your children. I heard from your son last summer through his sister-in-law and I am as a result gathering letters and plan to send photocopies when I have finished my search. (My house is full of papers.) It is a very good idea to write about Chaps. He was a marvellous personality but you know that − Dear Margaret − better than anybody.

"When he was very ill, in a letter, (Maybe the last?) that he wrote to me he told me that he was teaching you all about money and Banks and so on for the time when he would be here no more.... and he was so light-hearted about it all. What courage he had!

"I should like to see you again, Dear Margaret. Perhaps one day I shall cross the channel and come and see you.

"With our best wishes to you all. I think of you and say you my love,
    Gilberte."

CHAPTER 14

COMMANDER IN CHIEF
INDIAN AIR FORCE

Biographical Notes. Return to Peacetime.

*I returned to England in 1945 after a short spell as a POW in Germany
and following a bit of leave and some 'Rehabilitation' in hospital I was
promoted to Air Vice Marshal and given command of No 38 Group at
Marks Hall in Essex. During the war No 38 Group's function had been to
give Royal Air Force backing to Airborne Forces; towing the gliders and
providing air transport for paratroops. With the war over our task was
largely to keep in touch with the land forces scattered all over Europe from
Athens to Oslo, taking them their mail and newspapers and supplying air
transport as troops became due for de-mob. This gave me the excuse for
flying all over Europe and, on one occasion through to India, visiting on the
way the 6th Airborne Division in Palestine. But the main order of the day
was the running down of units, early demobilization and a general desire
to get the RAF back on to a smaller and more permanent footing. In the
course of this I was told to find a more stable home for my Group than the
requisitioned mansion in Essex that was its current home. The next day I
flew down to Salisbury Plain, having a soft spot for that part of the world
since my pre-war days there. RAF Upavon had just been declared available
for peacetime occupation so I grabbed it, and 38 Group and its successors
were resident at that famous old grass airfield for many years after. The
AOC's Residence at Marks Hall was nothing more than a couple of Prefabs
knocked together and planted in the grounds of the old Mansion. Much
grander and more comfortable was Littlecote House which went with the job
at Upavon.*

*After about 18 months of that I was hauled back to the Air Ministry
again or rather to Whitehall where I was the RAF Member of an inter-
service group known as the Defence Research Policy Staff. I won't explain
here exactly how we functioned or what we achieved, but the one great
'Spill off' was to bring me into close and almost daily contact with that great
man of science Sir Henry Tizard who at the time was chief scientific adviser
to the Ministry of Defence.*

142

From the DRPS I was posted in September 1948 on to the Directing Staff of the Imperial Defence College in Belgrave Square, then under the command of General Bill Slim. The Directing Staff of the IDC lead a very gentlemanly life; my ruder contemporaries dubbed it the Greatest Loaf in London. One of its great advantages was the opportunity to meet, argue with, and pick the brains of a large number of prominent men in all walks of life who came to address the students. These included politicians, economists, historians, leaders of Industry and Commerce, editors and journalists, leaders of religion and the great National and Commonwealth personalities of the day. In particular I recall the talks given by Field Marshal Smuts, The Dean of Westminster Cathedral, Harold Macmillan, Ernest Bevin and Professor Blackett.

Following my normal tour at the IDC I was given the exciting news that I was being loaned for a couple of years to the Indian Government to help run the Indian Air Force in the rank of Air Marshal.

Before examining Chaps' writings from India we should briefly examine what a Commander in Chief actually does in peacetime. When a country is not at war a military leader devotes his attention to implementing the policies of his political masters in preparation for any hostilities in prospect. With regard to the day-to-day running of a country's armed forces a Commander in Chief's role is more difficult to define. It is not much of an over-simplification to suggest that a C in C is there because an Army or an Air Force can not operate without one. The whole pyramid of military discipline requires one man at the pinnacle. Military operations require instant decisions that are impossible if an Army is led by a committee.

In wartime a military commander reaches his eminent position by selection and stays there by constant examination of his success. The decisions he makes have to be correct; the strategy has to be sound and battles have to be won. Morale needs to be high and the men who are doing the fighting have to look up to him with that mixture of admiration, respect and love that makes soldiers so pathetically vulnerable when things start going wrong.

In peacetime the examination of commanders is less harsh. The successful leader needs to project an image that inspires confidence. 'If it comes to a showdown the Boss'll see us right,' say the soldiers, and it is that condition, that need to foretell how 'The Boss' will behave if war breaks out that accounts for a lot of the drama and theatricality that surrounds the role of peacetime Commander in Chief. The scrambled eggs on the hat, the rank badges, the medals all proclaim the man's experience. The aura of hustle and impatience that surrounds inspections and parades, the carefully cultivated impression of omniscience, bluffness, aggression, even devices like the wearing of two cap badges are all carefully planned to demonstrate to the rank and file that in the event of hostilities it is inconceivable that 'The Boss' could be a loser. And if we are considering Air Force Commanders, it usually helps if they fly a lot.

The notion of Secondment is one that also needs examination. In previous centuries, fighting men who served countries other than their homeland, soldiers working for money without the spur of patriotism, were known as mercenaries. In a lot of ways a professional military man seconded to a foreign government was in a similar position. Military law and discipline are harsh enough when they are imposed for the benefit and protection of one's own homeland but the seconded man has to abide by the military code of an alien country and a country that, in many cases, has been in open conflict with his own. It requires enormous tact and flexibility to serve in another man's Air Force, even if you are ostensibly the Commander-in-Chief. Orders must give way to suggestions, reprimands to advice and the biblically impossible notion of serving two masters must become an every-day reality.

Two years after Independence India still had British Officers in her armed forces, ostensibly to lend their experience in the build-up of her own defence. In reality the Indians were not short of experienced fighting men, but what they really needed were senior officers who were patently unbiased in the tragic religious and racial conflict that was as divisive in the Armed Forces as in the rest of the country. Air Marshal Ivelaw-Chapman was an inspired choice for the post of Commander-in-Chief of the Indian Air Force. He had served and fought already in British India and was fascinated by the country and its people. While he remained a dedicated supporter of the British Way, he realized that the days of the Empire in India were over and felt that Great Britain had a remaining duty to nurture and defend the group of new-formed nations that had taken its place. It was valuable too that he and Margaret were a couple of great charm who captivated political high society in Delhi. They served as a reminder to the Indians that things were not all bad in the days of the Raj.

Biographical Notes. AOC in C Indian Air Force 1950-51.

I must include in this series of Service Memories some reference to my happy and eventful couple of years in India, after Independence, when I was loaned by the British Government to the Indian Government as the Commander in Chief of their Air Force. I was the penultimate Britisher to hold this post which I found most intriguing, bringing me as it did into close contact with a number of intelligent and personable Indians from Pandit Nehru downwards.

This was Margaret's first taste of life East of Suez and she took to it like a duck to water. She handled the servants well, was a marvellous hostess and very soon our circle of friends out there among all nationals was greatly enlarged thanks to her presence. She came with me on every tour of inspection that I made and we managed to see a large number of the more interesting places in India.

But to return to the Indian Air Force side of the picture; one of my earliest decisions was that one could not exercise proper command of such a widely spread force as was the IAF merely by sitting in an office in Delhi attending Chiefs of Staff Committees at the Defence Ministry and by representing the IAF at the unceasing flow of social engagements that Delhi indulged and delighted in. So I made it clear to my staff that I regarded 10 consecutive days as the maximum that I should spend in my Delhi office and that in consequence they should always have ready for me a provisional tour of outlying units that would keep me away for about a week. It didn't always work out with this mathematical precision but the net result was that there wasn't a single unit in the Indian Air Force, however small, that I did not visit at least once during my tour. This suited me fine as it gave me (and Margaret during the time that she was in India), the opportunity to visit most of the interesting places in the whole sub-continent. In all during my time in India I did 58 trips away from Delhi.

Another important conclusion that I came to soon after taking over was that too many of the IAF senior officers were content to become 'Chair-borne' and float along on their reputation that they had once qualified for their 'Wings'. Instead of gathering them all at a conference and ranting at them on the subject I resorted to a subtle — and for me pleasanter — form of attack. I discovered that in their photo reconnaissance unit they had a number of Spitfires with the Griffon engine (the Mark XXI I believe). Although I hadn't flown that particular Mark of Spitfire I mugged up on Pilot's Notes and within a few weeks of my arrival I used to sneak off to Palam airfield before breakfast and have half an hour or so of sheer pleasure flying one of these Spitfires. The effect was electric and precisely as I had intended. Soon some of the more elderly officers were clocking up flying hours in one or another aircraft of their own choosing. Next I took to arriving by Spitfire to take a passing out parade or a C in C's inspection. My ADC flew in formation with me in another Spit., and I had to undergo the ordeal of landing first in front of a vast parade drawn up on the tarmac, and usually a host of parents and official visitors as well. I managed to get away with it and just before the end of my tour I flew one of their Jets, the De Havilland Vampire with which they had just become equipped. This pleased them enormously and on the eve of my departure for England, at a rather formal ceremony in Delhi, I was presented by the Minister of Defence with Indian Air Force Wings thus bringing my total with the RFC and RAF up to 3.

Yet another conclusion that I reached was that if the Indian Air Force was to play its proper role in the Far East as a whole it had to make itself known and seen outside the confines of India itself. Consequently after I had played myself in, I led missions to Thailand, Burma, Malaya, Ceylon, Singapore and even to Car Nicobar. This was an excellent way of giving vent to my insatiable wanderlust and at the same time, I hope, doing the Indian Air Force a bit of good.

When I heard from the Air Ministry that I was to return to the UK in December 1951 to take up the post of Deputy Chief of the Air Staff I sat down and spread myself over 3 pages of foolscap pleading that I should be allowed to stay in India for another year "To finish off the job that I had begun," as I think I put it. To this I got but short shrift from CAS (Jack Slessor). His reply was to the effect that it was high time Chaps finished gallivanting round India in his Spitfire and came back to Whitehall and got down to some real *work.*

Sir Jack Slessor had probably got the measure of one part of Chaps' contribution to the fledgling Air Force of Independent India; namely that his obsession for getting everyone, himself included, into the air as much as possible, was in part self-indulgent. That he succeeded in persuading a lot of the senior officers in Air Headquarters in Delhi to fly was plain to see, but to what extent that policy in itself was beneficial has become increasingly open to doubt. For 'chairborne' pilots on staff duties to fly regularly is not a remotely cost-effective exercise in peacetime or indeed in war. The aircraft that are flown by pilots not on full time flying duties, the fuel that they burn and the groundcrew that they use for maintenance could and should all be more profitably used on operational or training flying for front-line squadrons. In the matter of safety it is a recognized factor in military aviation that pilots need to be 100 per cent familiar with their aircraft and that unless they fly at intervals of not greater than one week, efficiency and flying competence drops dramatically. Consider Chaps 'gallivanting round India in his Spitfire'. We read that the three Spitfires — one for the C in C, one for the ADC and at least one spare — were withdrawn from an IAF reconnaissance unit. Could this unit still operate and supply its quota of high level intelligence photography and mapping, if its aircraft and presumably its groundcrew were based at Palam on standby for the Chief's next unexpected visit? And, if anything went wrong with the aircraft or perhaps the weather, could the 51-year-old Air Marshal, with only about 30 widely scattered hours on type, cope with the emergency, or if the radio failed and communication with the ground was lost could he navigate well enough round the vast and unfamiliar country to find his way home?

146

Biographical Notes. Anecdotes. A Spitfire at Delhi.

On one occasion whilst I was Commander in Chief of the Indian Air Force during 1950, I flew down from Delhi to Agra in a Spitfire XXI to inspect the IAF unit stationed there. My ADC formated alongside me in another Spitfire. The ceremonial inspection over, I flew back to headquarters that evening. In the circuit, preparatory to landing, I moved the cockpit lever for lowering the undercarriage in the normal way, but the lever jammed solid half way through its quadrant and the green lights signifying that the wheels were locked down did not come on. There was a chemical bottle for generating gas under pressure for forcing down the undercarriage mechanism in just such an emergency, but according to Pilot's Notes this bottle should only be used if the control lever was fully down and nothing that I could do would move it. I got an Indian Air Force pilot who was very experienced on the Spitfire to come to the control tower and we discussed the problem. We agreed that I should activate the emergency bottle irrespective of the position of the control lever. I heard something mechanical happening beneath my seat but still there were no green lights. I flew low over the tower and they reported that the main wheels were down but there was no way of checking that they were locked. I was now short of fuel and could not stay in the air much longer so squaring up to the laws of gravity and the inescapable fact that what goes up must come down I turned in and landed. The main wheels were OK but the tail wheel had stayed locked up. This gave a fine display of sparks as the Spitfire settled down and its rear fuselage metal members scraped their way along the tarmac.

Another 'hairy' moment which Chaps seems to have survived with his usual combination of skill and good fortune, but imagine the disruption and consternation that this incident must have caused on the ground at what was already Delhi's international airport. So while Chaps clearly convinced himself that he was leading by example in cajoling the unwilling senior staff officers of the Indian Air Force into the air, in reality we must conclude that he was grabbing an unrepeatable opportunity to enjoy himself. What man with flying in his blood could have resisted the opportunity to career around the sky in the most powerful of the Spitfires, totally unrestrained by flying restrictions, Air Traffic Control and the scrutiny of superior officers? There were no superior officers.

It has been stated that Commanders in Chief quite rightly consider that they are expected to be a little theatrical if not downright eccentric in their behaviour. The bee in Chaps' bonnet was probably his obsession with flying and he can not really be faulted for that. The *Observer* newspaper's

Delhi correspondent noted some other peculiarities of the British Commanders in Chief on the Indian sub-continent in the early days of Independent India.

Article in a Canadian magazine by Rawle Knox datelined New Delhi.

THE ENIGMA OF SIX COMMANDERS.

"India and Pakistan, who currently live at a tension which any awkward incident might snap into war, allow five of the six commands of their respective armies, navies and air forces to rest in the hands of Britons. Who are the men who wear such uneasy responsibility? And is their presence any guarantee of peace on the Indo-Pakistan sub-continent?

"Perhaps the most whimsical and unorthodox of the group is the bulky, bespectacled, 46 year-old Air Vice-Marshal Bob Atcherley who commands the Pakistani Air Force. 21 years ago Atcherley was helping Britain win the Schneider Trophy outright by putting up a closed circuit flying record of 323½ mph. 'You need to be a little ostentatious in the East,' Atcherley claims.

"As an example he mentions the jet black, 30 foot high bomb which he has had erected outside his Karachi house. 'That's what I mean', said Atcherley. 'Generals will put guns outside their houses and I had to outdo them.'

"Pakistanis admire Atcherley's quality which they understand is inseparable from his eccentricities. His staff officers sometimes find their hair standing on end when they experience his breakneck flying, but they respect the drive which has set up Air Scout organizations and University Air Squadrons on the British model, and by doing so has stolen a march on India.

"Atcherley's opposite number, Air Marshal Ronald Ivelaw-Chapman is a more urbane, more studious type who continually surprises you with his knowledge of odd corners of the country whose Air Force he has been commanding for only a few months. But, like Atcherley, he is no chairborne officer. Flying his own Spitfire on surprise visits, the tall, slim air marshal, his hair almost ungreying despite his 51 years, keeps the Indian Air Force an enviably alert body.

The two men know each other well, attend Commonwealth conferences together and argue amicably about the advantages and disadvantages of attack over defence. For Atcherley is a fighter man and Ivelaw-Chapman a bomber. Does the distinction make any difference as far as India and Pakistan are concerned? I doubt it. 'If

148

India should attack us', Atcherley said to me once, 'at least we could bomb the hell out of Calcutta.' But I think he was joking.

Biographical Notes. People and Places. Pandit Nehru.

My last tour in India (1949-1951), was after 'Partition' and I was the servant of the Indian Government. As Commander in Chief of the Indian Air Force I was a member of the Indian Defence Committee. In that capacity, during my tour there I saw a lot of the first Indian ruler following Independence, Pandit Nehru. There were so many different sides to his character that I find it difficult to compress into a short space an adequate pen picture of that great, but not faultless man.

His outstanding trait was his magnetism. He could sway crowds by his oratory in a number of different Indian languages. His English was impeccable, eloquent and sincere. With these attributes he was able to cement together a sub-continent of millions of people who by nature, religion, climate and language were in fact a diverse and often opposed conglomeration of small nations. I once asked him his idea of a relaxed holiday. His reply staggered me. "To address a large concourse of people — preferably hostile."

As a Kashmiri Brahmin he was aristocratic and reserved. There were times in conversation when he did not listen at all when his mind was on other things. But on occasions he could be an engaging extrovert who was genuinely interested in all around him. He had a keen sense of humour and often delighted to poke fun, good-humouredly, at some of his colleagues in politics.

Like so many great men he had his blind spot. On one occasion, in company with many of his senior military and political advisers, I dined at his house. After dinner he discoursed at length on his impressions gained from a world tour that he had just completed that included a visit to the United States. For a while it was like listening to a great world statesman on a par with Eden or Smuts. His views on current affairs, both political and sociological in America, Europe and the Middle East, were expressed with wisdom and a rare balance of judgement. Then he got nearer to home as he turned to Indo-Pakistan relations. His whole manner changed and, in my view, he descended from the realms of statesmanship to that of a petty narrow-minded politician. Maybe it was because he hailed from Kashmir himself, or maybe there was some other reason, but whenever the conversation got around to the dispute with Pakistan over Kashmir he seemed to me to become quite irrational.

"Could the Air Force guarantee air superiority over a land battle in Kashmir?" Nehru asked me as coffee was being served. I was, to a degree, prepared for this question because his thoughts had been drifting inexorably

towards a military operation against Pakistan in the disputed Kashmir border area.

"I would rather not express an opinion on that matter, Sir," I replied, "because, as I have already confirmed to you, in the event of hostilities breaking out with Pakistan, it would be apparent that you had disregarded my strongest advice and I would be forced to resign from my Command."

If I had expected a rebuke or an argument to arise from this well-rehearsed and slightly insubordinate statement I was mistaken. Nehru's mind was already on another subject by the time I had finished speaking.

"Gandhi-jee used to say that there will be a peaceful transition to majority rule in southern Africa, but I don't think so. I feel there will be much blood-letting. What do you think, Menon?"

It always astounded me how devoid he was of any rancour against Britain despite the fact that he had spent 12 years of his life either in gaol or in house arrest under the regime of a British Government. He had an almost sentimental nostalgia for his days at Harrow and at Cambridge. Frequently after dinner his guests were taken below to his projection room and shown his own filming of English scenes and particularly of the 'Backs' at Cambridge.

It is reasonable to conclude that Chaps made a real contribution in the early days of Indian Independence to the nation's survival and development. We must remember that over a million citizens of India and Pakistan perished in the violence that followed the departure of the British. That such a disaster could have taken place without a formal declaration of war is an indication of the unthinking hatred that was still seething below the surface wherever Hindu came into direct confrontation with Moslem.

Ivelaw-Chapman's directive from the UK government in 1949 was to line up the Indian Air Force against communist expansionism from Russia and China to the north and to steer Nehru's country towards a useful defensive role in the anti-communist treaty organizations that were being negotiated at the time. What a gap there would have been in the West's defences if, at some time when the Cold War was only just being kept cold, India and Pakistan dissipated their strength in a war with each other. So Chaps with his Spitfire and Batchy Atchy with his bomb at the garden gate contributed significantly to world peace by their refusal to sanction even the notion that their respective Air Forces should set their sights on each other.

Anecdote. The Banyan Tree.

A new Indian Air Force Base was opened. The airfield and all the associated buildings were to be inspected by Jawarhalal Nehru, the Prime Minister. It was an occasion of flypasts, parades and much garlanding. The Commander in Chief was naturally at the Prime Minister's right hand during the formal ceremonies and Lady Ivelaw-Chapman and the sari-clad ladies of the new Base attended a great luncheon in the Mess.

After lunch the Prime Minister was scheduled to drive a few miles to a nearby town where a school building was to be opened. The ladies rose from the table a little before the Prime Minister's departure and made their way demurely to another place as ladies had been doing in Indian Mess life for the past 200 years. Margaret Ivelaw-Chapman admits that she found these ladies-only sessions rather trying in India largely because the English tongue was by no means universal amongst the wives. On this occasion she was relieved to be summoned from a gathering that had already lapsed into awkward silence, to attend Prime Minister Nehru. He was just stepping into his limousine to proceed to the school opening when he decided that he would like Lady Ivelaw-Chapman to accompany him.

They set off along about 15 miles of dusty road to the village where the school was to be opened. They talked of world affairs and philosophy, of England and India and of the loneliness of High Places.

"I'm enjoying talking to you so much that I think we'll stop for a moment," said the Prime Minister and gestured the driver to pull off the road into the shelter of a Banyan tree.

"Won't we be late?" asked Margaret.

"Probably," answered Nehru, "but it doesn't matter. Punctuality isn't so important now that the British have left India. Do you think the school would stay closed if I didn't turn up to open it? Of course not. Now let me tell you the story of the Banyan tree. You see how the roots descend to the earth from the branches; there is a parallel there in village life..."

The Prime Minister was amused by the consternation Margaret's presence caused at the school opening. Who was the tall elegant European woman at Nehru's side? Should she be seated with him while the children danced? Should she be garlanded? Should she be offered green tea and samosas? Surely she wasn't...royalty?

Two hours later Margaret was back at the Air Force Base. Chaps meanwhile had been taking his part in the traditional post-luncheon men-only gathering in the Officers' Mess, – port and cigars and stories considered unsuitable for ladies. He was just wondering with his ADC "What the Devil can have happened to her," when she appeared, slightly dusty and very amused.

"Remind me to tell you about the Banyan tree," she said. "It's fascinating how the roots go right down to the ground from the branches. That's the way it renews itself you know. We can see a parallel there with village life."

CHAPTER 15

MAN OF INFLUENCE

Biographical Notes. The Sunset of My Service Career.

During my last few weeks in India I contracted a disease the origins of which defeated the Indian Doctors and, for a time, those at home in England. I had some form of creeping paralysis which affected my speech, taste and swallow. I flew home in pretty poor shape just before Christmas in 1951 and went straight into Halton RAF Hospital. After a few days there I was taken to the National Hospital for Nervous Diseases in London. The paralysis gradually spread until I had no feeling in my hands and feet and little control over my speech and swallowing muscles. After being subjected to a number of painful and rude examinations it was established that I was suffering from an obscure polyneuritis akin to diphtheria. The disease finally started to retreat but not before I was faced with the horrifying prospect of becoming an alert vegetable. After 5 or 6 months in hospital I came out 98% restored to health and took up a new post as Commander in Chief of Home Command based at White Waltham. After only about 7 months there I was summoned back to the Air Ministry as Deputy and later Vice Chief of the Air Staff with a seat on the Air Council and there I remained for the next 4½ years until I retired from the Service in 1957. In the context of this journal there is but little to record of this exacting period. Plenty of hard work, plenty of knotty problems to solve, plenty of 'Dining Out' and 'Lunching Out' for the RAF and plenty of contact with the leaders of the other two Services, with Cabinet Ministers, with the Press and with the Magnates of the Aircraft Industry.

Looking back over those years I wonder how I survived the terrific tempo of the life I led with nearly every moment of the day booked and a spate of evening formal engagements to end off an exacting day in the office. But I have nothing to complain of. In fact I am extremely grateful that the summit of my career found me in such an important and influential position with friends all round me and a willing wife to share the burden.

That is the final entry under the Memories section in Chaps' biographical Memories and Musings volumes. The aim of these editorial notes has been to show how in Chaps' life his experiences formed his opinions or, in other words, the influence of the Memories upon the Musings. It is during the period of his life now under consideration that his opinions and convictions were important because he had reached a position of sufficient eminence in public life to have some influence on the way things were done.

It is also significant that his views on a wide variety of subjects were not his alone but were broadly shared by the Edwardian Military Gentleman class who, although they rarely entered the political arena, nevertheless had a considerable influence on national affairs in the 25 years 1950 — 1975. The Musings show the general thoughts of men like Sir Ronald and I have tried to summarize a few examples of the philosophy that he so laboriously recorded.

His views on atomic warfare are considered in rather more detail because the establishment of the British deterrent was probably this generation of military men's greatest contribution to the world order today.

He devoted much of his thinking to re-assessing the Seven Deadly Sins in his own particular order of deadliness. It was his rather gentle version of the popular fantasy, "Who will face the firing squad after my revolution?" He came to no firm conclusion but decided that Lust had had rather a bad press and on the whole was considerably less deadly than Greed which he put at the head of the list, followed closely by Envy and Hatred. These three, he wrote, were the cause of every war that he had read about or been involved in. He was surprisingly tolerant of Sloth which came at the bottom of his list. He didn't admire or tolerate laziness, but, in common with the men of his generation, he judged a sin by the amount of pain it inflicted on others, and on those grounds there wasn't a lot wrong with a bit of Sloth every now and then.

How enviably simple is this classification of the Deadly Sins. Would a man reach a similar position of eminence in Britain today if he was guided by the notion that Greed was the deadliest sin and that it was of great importance not to engage in any activity that inflicted pain or discomfort on other people?

He argued convincingly that the great benefit of the advent of manned military aviation during the First World War was that it eliminated once and for all the notion that civilians could distance themselves from the misery and madness of war by paying the military to do the fighting for them. From the first Zeppelin raid onwards, no one was safe once hostilities had been declared. He expanded this idea with optimism which might surprise people who imagine that the Edwardian Military were just fighting automatons who did nothing but carry out orders.

Biographical Notes. The Musings. Thoughts on Military Aviation.

I personally incline to the view that the elimination of 'Civilians' in our strategic thinking is to the advantage of mankind rather than the reverse. For it makes every one of us more politically conscious and more critical of the decisions made by those whom we vote into power. It thus makes less likely the prospect of another global affray.

I am convinced too that, despite all the inhumanities of the two Japanese atomic attacks, mankind should be grateful that the war with Japan did not end before the power of the airborne atom bomb had been practically demonstrated. If Japan had been defeated earlier and if the atom bomb as a military weapon had been left as a matter of conjecture to be argued about ad nauseam by scientists, professional and amateur strategists and by politicians, we might well have seen a third global conflagration.

Top Secret Report on a Visit to the Soviet Union in June 1956. (The distribution list indicates that it was read by the Prime Minister, the Cabinet and the whole of the Air Council. A copy, complete with scarlet security stamp, is pasted into one of the scrap books.)

1. GENERAL

It was abundantly clear from the start of the visit that the Soviet hierarchy had issued strict instructions that Friendship and Co-operation were to be the keynote. This was evidenced by the lavishness of the hospitality, the apparent warmth of our reception, the trouble taken to meet our wishes for sight-seeing, the readiness with which they answered most of our questions and the openness with which they displayed their current equipment including armament, bomb-sights and radar. It was also clear that the British and American Missions were singled out for pride of place amongst the other missions in all respects. This confirms my long-held view that the Russian leadership respect our nuclear capability and we would be delegated to an unacceptably lowly position in any negotiations if we did not have our own independent nuclear strike force.

2. THEIR PLANS

Even if in response to the need for raising the standard of living of the masses, which, outside the privileged class, still appears appallingly low, there must be a re-adjustment of the 'Guns to Butter' ratio, it will not be the Soviet Air Force that suffers. We may ask why they spend money and resources on both the offensive and defensive aspect of military aviation if they do not intend to trigger off a global war themselves. My estimate is that they have no such intention; they are far too aware of America's and latterly our growing nuclear power. No, their purpose in striving to become a first-class nuclear armed air power strikes me as being three-fold:

    a. To eliminate for ever the fear of America or ourselves starting a preventative war against them — a possibility that may sound remote enough to us but is a real fear to those in the Kremlin.

    b. To form an umbrella, as it were, under which they can, without too much risk of retaliation, follow up the successes they have achieved in recent years in their conduct of the Cold War and their penetration into the Middle East and elsewhere.

    c. Finally, to give themselves a politico/strategic bargaining counter.

3. CONCLUSION

It is therefore my conclusion that we are handling the very real threat of Soviet Nuclear Capability in the right manner. Our aim must be to match them, in conjunction with, but independently of the Americans in every step of the way to Nuclear Air Power. They must be aware that the West can not be surprised and will not be deflected from its determination to use nuclear weapons if world peace is threatened. In these circumstances I am confident that nuclear war will remain only a threat, and that in the not too distant future the nuclear confrontation will end simply because the Soviet Union hasn't the resources properly to maintain it.

Signed R I-C
VCAS.
1 July, 1956.

Sir Ronald was more than an articulate verbal supporter of the British independent nuclear deterrent. During his time as a policy maker, the Royal Air Force embarked on a long and honourable period as the operators of Britain's strategic nuclear strike force. The British-made V-Bombers went on standby at readiness states calculated in minutes. They operated from bunkers at bases as widespread as Gan in the Maldive Islands, Singapore and Aden as well as the East Anglian airfields in this country. The bombs which were slung in their bomb bays, needing only a secret code to arm them, were British-made and of course the pilots who manned the aircraft and occasionally took them all the way to the Iron Curtain on practice scrambles were Britons, loyal successors to the aircrew who served us so gallantly in the Second World War.

Had we not followed Chaps' life story from his first spluttering flights in the Royal Flying Corps it might seem paradoxical that a man who listed Hatred as one of the most deadly of sins, who searched his heart over the problems and social needs of the underprivileged in this and other lands, who applauded family life and who had often shown himself capable of genuinely loving his enemy, could throw his weight behind such a policy of total destruction. But the Edwardian Military Gentlemen had a facility to conduct wars without hatred and they could equate the tenderest of feelings with daily consideration of death by megaton and mushroom cloud. Indeed it is difficult to imagine any other leaders who could have trained and motivated their men to the point where to unleash a nuclear war was a matter of turning one more switch and flying a hundred or so miles further along the same course, and at the same time to carry the personal conviction that the final irrevocable step was never actually going to be taken. And now that the Cold War is over and won we can not but applaud the vision and determination of the men who led us through those early terror-filled years.

It has been demonstrated that Ivelaw-Chapman, in all roles and ranks from 2nd Lieutenant Royal Flying Corps to Air Chief Marshal, Vice Chief of Air Staff, had a notable loyalty to his Country and Sovereign. This final story shows his loyalty to the British Constitution and, in passing, sheds light on the so-called plot to destabilize the Government of Harold Wilson in the mid-1970s. If people realized the impossibility of mobilizing the Edwardian Military Gentlemen in an anti-government coup, however dissatisfied they were with the current incumbent of No 10 Downing Street, credence would not have been given to the unlikely suggestions that such a plot had taken place. The author of *Spycatcher*, who definitely was not an Edwardian Military Gentleman, would have been quite properly laughed out of court instead of being profitably and unsuccessfully prosecuted.

The Bath Service Luncheon. May 1975. Ivelaw-Chapman Folklore.

The cast list for the Ceremony of the Installation of the Great Master and Knights Grand Cross of the Most Honourable Order of the Bath was impressive. At 10.40 o'clock a detachment of Her Majesty's Bodyguard of the Honourable Corps of Gentlemen at Arms entered Westminster Abbey. The Great Master, Prince Charles, followed shortly afterwards and a few minutes later Her Majesty the Queen entered by the West Door. The Canons and Choristers of Westminster were there, the Band of the Welsh Guards and the Trumpeters of the Royal Military School of Music. The address was to be delivered by the Archbishop of Canterbury and Primate of All England. The Gentleman Usher of the Scarlet Rod had his place in the Procession, as did Bath King of Arms and the Dean of the Order carrying the Oath and the Admonition 'Fairly engrossed upon vellum'.

The full complement of Knights Grand Cross, including those to be installed, slowly and somewhat infirmly walked down the aisle with their burgundy mantles lending unfamiliar panache to the slightly stooped shoulders of the Grand Old Men of Great Britain who were being honoured in this essentially British ceremony. The names of the Knights read like a catalogue of the Edwardian Military Gentlemen. Most of them were aged at least 75 but even those who needed Pages and black-uniformed Ushers to help them mount the chancel steps exuded an air of military uprightness that made outsiders wonder, and imagine what men they must have been in their Prime.

Knights Grand Cross to be Installed:

Field Marshal Sir Richard Hull, GCB, DSO, DL. General the Lord Bourne, GCB, KBE, DSO. General Sir Dudley Ward, GCB, KBE, DSO, DL. Field Marshal Sir Francis Festing, GCB, KBE, DSO, DL. Air Chief Marshal Sir Harry Broadhurst, GCB, KBE, DSO, DFC, AFC. Admiral Sir William Davis, GCB, DSO, DL. Air Chief Marshal Sir Ronald Ivelaw-Chapman, GCB, KBE, DFC, AFC. Marshal of the Royal Air Force Sir Dermot Boyle, GCB, KCVO, KBE, AFC.

After the Service in Westminster Abbey the Knights and their families and attendants dispersed to their various London Clubs for Luncheon. The dining room of the RAF Club was filled with uniforms as never before except in wartime. Chaps' party consisted of his wife, his sister Eileen and his son and daughter and Tony Shortt who had attended the Service as a Companion and now, dressed in his General's uniform, joined the RAF party in the elegant building in Piccadilly.

The conversation was, in the main, light-hearted but towards the end of the meal it was inevitable that the subject was raised of Harold Wilson and the current Labour administration. This Government was much disdained by the Edwardian Military Gentlemen. It is not hard to understand why. Many essentially British institutions were under attack. Ultimate power seemed to be slipping away from Westminster into the irresponsible and ungentlemanly hands of the Trade Unions. The Pound Sterling was under attack, the Empire was being given away. There was sympathy for Ian Smith, himself a distinguished ex-RAF man, and the Rhodesian rebellion, and a scurrilous Labour MP apparently considered it his duty regularly to denounce the Queen.

It was Tony Shortt who raised the subject of direct action.

"Why don't we do something about it ?" he said. "Surely there's enough Leadership among the likes of us to organize a little pressure to get rid of that beggar Wilson and get the country back on a proper footing. I hear the cloak and dagger merchants are looking for some one at the top of the Services to stand up and be counted, if you know what I mean." Those present, who were sufficiently mellowed by the wine and overawed by the uniforms to agree with anything, agreed. Chaps remained silent and the talk veered away to less contentious matters.

"Funny to think that the fat old Air Marshal at the next table with the seven rows of medals was once known as 'Dingbat'."

But Chaps was thinking, and about two or three subjects later he interrupted whatever exchange was then in progress.

"They must be mad," he growled. The onset of deafness in old age caused him on occasions to speak a little louder than the situation required. The effect on this occasion was to grab the attention not only of those seated with him, but also of a number of people taking lunch at adjacent tables.

"Who must?" asked Tony.

"Any one who could imagine that one of us," and here Chaps gestured expansively with his Air Chief Marshal's uniformed arm to take in the great and the gallant in the room and those who stared down sternly from the portraits on the walls and all men who had lived and served as they had done; "Any one who could imagine that the likes of Us would ever support any sort of unconstitutional opposition to the Government of the Day must be insane." Tony Shortt, suddenly chastened, murmured that the suggestion had not been serious, but Chaps was now in full flow. "All this Chivalry business; the Grand Crosses and the Banners and the Service in the Abbey are not just for show. The Knights of the Bath have been selected from the most loyal supporters of the Sovereign and Constitution of the British Isles since the 15th century and it's not going to change now. It doesn't matter a damn whether we like the Government or not, we will always support it. The British Constitution can survive a few years of Harold Wilson."

Luncheon was over and with it probably the most triumphant occasion in Chaps' life. We filled our glasses once more with the Burgundy from Beaune and Chaps rose rather painfully to his feet and proposed the Loyal Toast. We all stood and so, quite spontaneously, did every other person in the room.

Biographical Notes. The Musings. "Introspection."

I can see that this 'Introspection' caper is running away with me and if I continue much longer I will only succeed in painting a picture of a priggish, conceited and self-righteous old gentleman. But I can't refrain from closing with a mention of one more quality which I can claim to possess and of which I am proud. This is Contentment. I am not self-content; I am content with my lot and have been at each stage throughout my life. I can well remember saying when I was still a Flight Lieutenant in 1932 that I would have done very well in the RAF if I ever reached the exalted rank of Group Captain. I could not have been happier than during my couple of years as C-in-C of the Indian Air Force and I really enjoyed my last 4 years in the Service as a member of the Air Council.

Now, in retirement I am supremely happy, with a wife who means more to me than any man deserves; with a lovely home and garden, a large circle of friends, a variety of village interests, 2 motor cars and an income that (just) allows us to entertain to the modest extent which we enjoy. Added to that I have recently come through a successful operation for colostomy, I have received 'Letters Patent' from Garter King of Arms granting Arms to myself and my family and I have the promise of a Stall in the Henry VII Chapel in Westminster Abbey where I hope to be installed in May 1975 and above which Stall is already placed my 'Achievement'. So who would not be content?

Signed R Ivelaw-Chapman.
Knockwood
Nether Wallop
December 1974.

INDEX

Kabul, Afghanistan, 52, 58, 59, 63, 64, 65, 67, 68, 69, 70, 71, 78
Karachi, 59, 62, 66
Kandahar, Afghanistan, 67
Khan, Ali Ahmed, Afghan Leader, 69, 70, 73, 74
Khan, Afzal, Indian Clerk, 76
Khan, Jehangir, Indian Consul, Jellalabad, 75
Kitchener's Army, 6
Kipling, Rudyard, 31, 40, 65, 73, 76, 78
Kirmington R.A.F. Station, 97
Killinger, Ober-Leutnant, 131, 133, 134
Kuwait, 52

L

Lancaster Aircraft, 11, 13, 93, 96, 97, 99, 100, 101, 106, 137, 140
Lawrence, T. E., 51, 55
Lahore, 66
Latoband Pass, Afghanistan, 67
Langley, Col., M.I.9., 103
Lecomte Family, French Resistance, 109, 110
Lincoln City, Lincolnshire, 13, 14, 49
Linton on Ouse, R.A.F. Station, 87, 88, 90, 91
Lucknow, India, 34, 35
Luftwaffe, 115
Ludlow-Hewitt, Sir Edgar, 84
Lydford, Air Marshal Sir Harold (Reggie), 12
Lysander Aircraft, 110, 136

M

Martlesham Heath R.A.F. Station, 41, 44, 46, 47, 80
Maxwell, Sqn. Ldr., R.A.F., 52, 67
Mark's Hall, R.A.F. Unit, 142
Macmillan, Harold, 143
Menin Airfield, Belgium, 27
Mesopotamia, 51
Messerschmidt 110 Aircraft, 101
'Meccano' Toy, 108, 139
Mosul, Iraq, 52, 53, 54
Morgan, General Sir Frederick, 95
Mosquito Aircraft, 100
Morton, Desmond, Prime Minister's secretary, 103
'Mrs. Dale's Diary', Radio Programme, 39
Murray, Major Keith, R.F.C., 15, 18, 45, 104
Mussolini, 88
Mulberry Harbour, 94

N

Napier Lion Aero Engine, 42, 62, 66, 70
Nasyriah, Iraq, 56
Najar, Jacoub, carpenter, 79
Nehru, Pandit Jawaharlal, ii, 144, 149, 150, 151
Nether Wallop, Hampshire, ii, 159
Netheravon R.A.F. Station, 81, 84
Neave, Airey, MP, 103, 104, 110, 114
News of the World, 114
North West Frontier Province, India, 59
North Weald R.A.F. Station, 80
North Killingholme R.A.F. Station, 97
North Coates R.A.F. gunnery range, 46, 47
Nuremburg War Crimes Trial, 132
Nuclear Power, 154

O

Oberursel village, Frankfurt, Germany, 122, 124, 125, 131
Over Wallop, Hampshire, 94
'OVERLORD' Codename, Invasion of Europe, 93, 96
Oxford, 7

P

Parnall Possum Aircraft, 42
Pasni, Baluchistan, 62
Patard Family, 108, 116, 139
Pakistan Air Force, 148
Pelota, Basque game, 52, 55
Peshawar India, 65, 66, 67, 70, 74, 78
Pir Sahib, Religious leader, 71, 74, 75, 78, 79, 127, 136
'PLUTO' Acronym, 94
Portal, Marshal of the R.A.F. Sir Charles, 84, 86
Prague, Czechoslovakia, 81
Pygmalion. Opera House, Cairo, 55

Q

Quetta, India, 64, 65

R

R.A.F. Club, 58, 128, 157
Ravensbruck Concentration Camp, Germany, 113
R.A.F. Escaping Society, 137
Rawle Knox, Journalist, 148
R.E.8. Aircraft, 8, 11
Red Cross, The, 106, 121, 130
Renée village, France, 107, 108, 116

164